THE EDGE OF OBLIVION

The Looming Threat of Socialism in the United States

by

Charles K. Kelly

Dorrance Publishing Co
585 Alpha Drive
Pittsburgh, PA 15238
Visit our website at *www.dorrancebookstore.com*

ISBN: 978-1-6491-3349-6
eISBN: 978-1-6491-3268-0

On
July 27, 1967

An American Patriot

Kenneth L. Hendrix
United States Army
Specialist Four

A Resident of Carriere, Mississippi

Made the Ultimate Sacrifice
While Serving His Country
In Vietnam

To His Honored Memory

This Book Is
Respectfully
Dedicated

Appreciation

I would like to express my most profound thanks to my good friend Professor Phillip Miller for his kindness and willingness to review my manuscript for this book in preparation for its submission for publication.

I would also like to express my heart-felt appreciation and thanks to Jill Kelly, my wife of almost thirty-two years, for her support and encouragement during the long hours of work and research that went into the writing of this book and the financial support required for its publication.

Last, but not least, I want to offer my thanks to

Almighty God

who blessed me with the reality of being born into such a country as the United States of America, where freedom is a reality and not a distant dream.

"The American people will never knowingly adopt socialism. But, under the name of 'liberalism,' they will adopt every fragment of the socialist program, until one day America will be a socialist nation, without knowing how it happened."

Norman Mattoon Thomas
(American Presbyterian minister, socialist, and six-time
presidential candidate for the Socialist Party of America.)

. . .

"There is no difference between communism and socialism, except in the means of achieving the same ultimate end: communism proposes to enslave men by force, social-ism – by vote. It is merely the difference between murder and suicide."

Ayn Rand (Alisa Zinovyevna Rosenbaum)
(Russian-American writer And philosopher)

. . .

"The last capitalist we hang shall be the one who sold us the rope."

Karl Marx
(Co-author of the Communist Manifesto)

. . .

"The problem with socialism is you eventually run out of other people's money."

Margaret Thatcher
(Former Prime Minister of Great Britain)

. . .

"There are only two places where socialism will work: Heaven, where they don't need it; and Hell, where they already have it."

Sir Winston Churchill
(Former Prime Minister of United Kingdom)

Introduction

The United States of America has stood as a free and independent nation for over two centuries. It has been attacked, invaded, terrorized, suffered varying degrees of social and political unrest, economic ups and downs, a variety of crises, hardships and heartaches, environmental disasters, and other dilemmas. However, this nation has remained free despite any obstacle faced by its citizens, people from multiple national and ethnic backgrounds, races, and creeds. The citizens of the United States have often agreed to disagree on many issues; however, when a threat to America rears its ugly head, the American people have stood together to face and overcome anything which posed a threat to their freedom and way of life.

But in the first quarter of the twenty-first century, a new and ominous threat to the freedom and way of life of the American people has risen from the chilling depths of disguise and openly revealed its presence, reality, and intentions. It is a threat which has already devastated numerous nations and countless individuals around the world, abolishing their freedom, their rights, their will, and, in many cases, even costing them their lives. A threat which, like a wolf in sheep's clothing, has never delivered what it promised, but rather has taken everything its proponents desired. A threat which offers an olive branch with one hand, while holding a whip in the other. A threat whose proponents care nothing for what they preach but desire only what they can inflict. A threat which will do anything to secretly or openly force its way into an inattentive or complacent society which has been blinded to this monster by its deceptive supporters who sing praises to its doctrine, the whole truth of which is never revealed to the unwary citizen until it is too late. A threat, which once firmly established is very costly, if not impossible to overthrow. That threat is SOCIALISM!

Chapter One

American History at a Glance

In 1534, King Henry VIII became disgruntled with the Roman Catholic Church due to the refusal of its leader, Pope Clement VII, to annul Henry's marriage to Catherine of Aragon, who had failed to provided Henry with a male heir. Unlike the Catholic Church of today, the Catholic Church of the Middle Ages was a powerful political entity. In response to the pope's refusal, King Henry VIII declared himself the head of a new national church, which became known as the Church of England.

The Protestant Reformation, which swept Europe in the sixteenth century, resulted in a break with the Catholic Church over power, ritualism, and other issues practiced under Medieval Catholicism. However, the Church of England retained many of these ritual practices which led many reformers to lose faith in the possibility of bringing worship back to the basics of the teachings of the Bible rather than the authoritative teachings of the Catholic Church of the Middle Ages.

Discouraged by the lack of change in church power and structure, and due to the fact that the authoritative nature of the Church of England bore little difference to the authoritative nature of its predecessor, a group of individuals in England made the decision to leave England for a fresh start in a new land. They were known as Puritans because of their desire to purify the Christian Church as a whole from secular heresy and corruption.

Over time, the Puritans became a persecuted group. During the reign of Henry VIII, it was a violation of the law to be a part of any congregation other than the Church of England. People who resisted the authority of the Church of England under King Henry VIII's leadership were punished with harassment, fines, and some were even imprisoned. When the Puritans saw there was little hope of change to their situation in England, they elected to leave England and settle in Holland.

However, life in Holland brought on new difficulties. Entire families were forced to work to make a living, and some Puritan children were lured away by the Dutch and enticed to serve in the army and navy of Holland. As hostilities between several European countries began to escalate, the Puritans became fearful a new war might possibly erupt between Holland and Spain, and after consulting with one another, the Puritans elected to move to the New World in North America and begin a new life.

In 1620, two small ships, the *Speedwell* and the *Mayflower*, set out from England bound for the New World. However, after twice turning back due to the *Speedwell's* observed unseaworthiness, the *Mayflower* sailed alone September 6, 1620, carrying 102 passengers. Sixty-six days later, after a perilous voyage, the *Mayflower* arrived in Plymouth in present day Massachusetts on November 11, 1620.

Before departing the ship, the Puritan leaders drafted and signed a document which would serve as a governing guideline for their colony. That document, which became known as the Mayflower Compact, emphasized the purpose of the Puritans' presence in the New World was to establish a home where they would be free to practice and share the Christian faith without the persecution, harassment, or interference of the Church of England.

The Puritans established relations with the local inhabitants: the Pakonoket Wampanoag Indians. The Indian leader, Massasoit, entered into a treaty with the Pilgrims which specified that neither the Pilgrims nor the Indians would attempt to harm one another, any wrongs committed would be handled by the guilty party's own people, the Indians and the Pilgrims would be allies in the event of a conflict with another hostile force, and no weapons would be present on either side during a time of meeting. The Indians and the Pilgrims lived and peace, and with one another's help, the Plymouth colony survived.

Over the years, more and more settlers arrived in the New World, and eventually, thirteen English colonies were established along the Eastern North American Coast. But interference from England continued. Taxes, the presence of armed troops, and other issues began to drive a wedge between the colonists and their mother country. Discontent continued to grow, disagreements increased, injustices occurred, and eventually, the volatile situation in the American colonies drifted past the point of no return.

In the early morning hours of April 19, 1775, approximately eighty patriots, armed only with their own personal weapons, stood their ground on the green of a small Massachusetts town called Lexington against nearly seven hundred regular infantrymen of the British army in defiance of tyranny. Some six years later, on October 19, 1781, their sacrifice was rewarded as the British army, under the command of General Cornwallis, met its defeat at the Battle of Yorktown at the hands of the Continental Army, commanded by General George Washington.

In 1786, Congress embarked upon a plan to draft a new constitution to replace the Articles of Confederation, which had served as the colonies' governing document during the American Revolution, and the Constitutional Convention convened at Independence Hall in Philadelphia, Pennsylvania on May 25, 1787, to begin their important work. After some three tedious months of work and debate, the forty-one delegates of the Constitutional Convention, which was moderated by George Washington, later to become the nation's first president, completed the draft of the Constitution on September 17, 1787. Article VII of the Constitution required that a minimum of nine of the thirteen states must ratify the Constitution for it to become a binding document. The document was initially signed by thirty-eight of the forty-one delegates of the Constitutional Convention.

The new government created by the Constitution set in place a strong federal government consisting of three branches: Executive, Legislative, and Judicial. This division of power established a system of checks and balances intended to keep power from becoming absolute, and from keeping either one person or a handful of individuals from wielding total power and authority; a government which was intended to be of the people, by the people, and for the people.

Beginning on December 7, 1787, five of the thirteen states quickly ratified the Constitution in quick succession. However, other states, including Massachusetts, withheld their support for the document because, in the eyes of their respective delegates, it failed to reserve undelegated powers to the states and lacked constitutional protection of what many of the constitutional delegates viewed as basic political rights, such as freedom of speech, religion, and the press. A compromise was reached under which Massachusetts and other states agreed to ratify the document with the understanding and assurance that amendments would be immediately proposed, and the Constitution was narrowly ratified by delegates from Massachusetts, Maryland, and South Carolina.

New Hampshire ratified the Constitution on June 21, 1788, becoming the ninth state to do so, and it was agreed that the government established under the United States Constitution would begin on March 4, 1789. Virginia ratified the Constitution in June of that same year, followed by New York the following month. On September 25, 1789, the first Congress of the United States of America adopted twelve amendments to the US Constitution and sent them to the states for ratification. The first ten amendments, which would become known as the Bill of Rights, were ratified in 1791. North Carolina became the twelfth state to ratify the Constitution in November.

The State of Rhode Island finally ratified the Constitution on May 29, 1790, and the last of the original thirteen colonies finally became an official part of the new nation which would become known as the United States of America. Nearly fifteen years after those first shots were fired at Lexington, Massachusetts, the Constitution of the United States of America became a reality, and today it stands as the oldest written constitutions still in use anywhere in the world.

For 229 years, the United States Constitution has served as the law of the land; however, in recent decades threatening storm clouds have been gathering on the horizon which threaten to either reduce or erase the freedoms guaranteed by this priceless work of legislation which millions of Americans have sworn to support and defend against all enemies, both foreign and domestic, and for which many individuals from colonial times until the present day have made the ultimate sacrifice in carrying out that sacred duty. Those storm clouds are the storm clouds of socialism.

The United States has never been, nor will it ever be, a *perfect* nation, because like all nations, it is populated by imperfect people. America has done many good and wonderful things for other peoples and other nations around the world. It has aided many countries with personnel, economic, and material assistance after their being struck by environmental disasters such as storms, earthquakes, famines, and so forth. The United States has sent its armed forces into harm's way to defend the rights of the oppressed around the world and has helped liberate many countries which have been overrun and occupied by hostile aggressors. America has provided medical and sustenance aid for the hungry and sick of countless nations, and over the years since its founding, the United States of America has rushed to help the helpless in ways which no other nation could or would.

America has pursued and accomplished many amazing and seemingly impossible endeavors, from landing men on the surface of the moon to sending probes beyond our own solar system into the vastness of interstellar space. Its scientists, doctors, and engineers have built upon one another's work and efforts to produce countless technical achievements: computers, which once took up entire buildings, have been reduced to small technical devices which fit easily into a small briefcase; diseases, which were once rampant killers, have been all but eradicated; catastrophic illnesses, which once meant a death sentence, are now being cured at an increasing rate; and personal communication, which once relied on the slow delivery of mail, may now be accomplished at the dial of a palm-sized, portable cell phone or the click of a send button for electronic mail.

But along with America's goodness and amazing achievements, there is a darker part of our history. Acts of unfairness and injustice which would seem to have no place in a society embraced by our Founding Fathers in which all men are said to be created equal. With its growth, expansion, and achievements, America has also inflicted many injustices both on other people and on the beautiful environment which stretches from sea to shining sea. Methyl mercury, a biproduct of refineries and certain power plants, has contaminated numerous rivers and streams, resulting in both costly environmental cleanup operations and countless health hazards. Improper disposal of garbage has created sanitation hazards, which in turn create illnesses in both humans as well as animals. The Passenger Pigeon, California Grizzly Bear, Cascade Mountains Wolf, Easter Elk, and other species have been driven into endangerment or extinction.

But worst of all is the negative impact of America on other human beings. The proud American Indian, who saved the Pilgrims from starvation when they first arrived on the shores of the North American continent, was later cheated, treated with distain, and betrayed time and time again. Negro men and women, kidnapped from their homelands in Africa, were brought across the Atlantic Ocean by ship and sold like animals as slaves. They were treated with contempt and persecuted for decades before their freedom was won.

Legal immigrants from other nations entered America in poverty, and many never rose above a low economic status despite their hard work and efforts.

However, from the well of imperfection, the United States has produced a remarkable people. People who have risen above unfairness and persecution to not only overcome the injustices of the past, but to contribute to a nation whose goodness outweighs its imperfections in the end. People who eventually came together regardless of race, color, creed, or differences of opinion to stand up to the challenges which threaten to impact the nation as a whole.

As Lewis and Clark trudged across North America exploring the Louisiana Purchase from 1804 to 1806, they were guided during part of their journey by a young Indian girl named Sacagawea.

During the War of 1812, General Andrew Jackson, as he faced discouraging odds in preparation to defend the city of New Orleans from the approaching British Army, found support and assistance from a privateer named Jean Lafitte.

In the closing days of World War I, a Battalion of American infantry composed mostly of young men of Jewish, Irish, Polish, and Italian decent, dug in and held off multiple attacks by the German army while cut off behind enemy lines, inflicting such a catastrophic loss on their enemy that the entire front was weakened, helping to bring what was called the *war to end all wars* to an end.

When the world erupted into a Second World War some twenty years later, a group of African American fighter pilots, who no senior officer would trust at first, put their frustrations and anger aside and demanded the right to fight for a nation which was just as much theirs as it was anyone else's. Their skill, daring, dedication to duty, and tenacious aggression in combat while protecting American bombers led to the Tuskegee Airmen being not only acknowledged as a reliable fighting unit, but actually requested by B-17 crews for bomber escort in the dangerous skies over Europe.

Japanese Americans—American citizens who were placed in internment camps out of fear because of their ancestry, demanded and won the right to serve and fight for *their* country. The Nisei (Japanese American) troops served with distinction in the European Theater of World War Two. One of many decorated Nisei soldiers, Medal of Honor recipient Daniel K. Inouye, lost his right arm while charging a German machinegun nest. He would later serve as a United States senator from Hawaii for forty-nine years, from 1963 until his death in 2012.

Navajo Indians answered America's call to serve as they joined the American armed forces and provided a means of secure communications based on their native language which no one else in the world knew or understood.

In the despairing days following the devastating terrorist attacks which occurred on September 11, 2001, attacks which took the lives of nearly three thousand American citizens, an entire country, despite the many differences and opinions of its citizenship, stood together in a united will to see those who planned and perpetrated this atrocity brought to justice. After a long and intense search lasting nearly two years, American intelligence operatives finally located the perpetrator of these attacks: Osama Bin Laden, the head of the al-Qaeda Terrorist Organization, at his hiding place in a compound located within the nation of Pakistan. In a daring move, then President Barak Obama issued an order sending United States military forces across the border of Pakistan in the dead of night, and in the ensuing action, the life of a terrorist long sought by the American people was brought to a quick and decisive end.

But the unity of America is rapidly becoming a thing of the past, and the America of today is a nation which is growing increasingly divided. This division is the result of the emergence of an increasing unwillingness for many emerging leaders to recognize, acknowledge, stand by, and defend the Constitutional Rights of those who disagree with them.

The Constitution of the United States was ratified only after certain rights were defined, guaranteed, and written into a series of amendments which would become known as the Bill of Rights.

A fact which many emerging leaders in the hallowed halls of the United States Government fail to acknowledge is that the Bill of Rights is a component of the ratified Constitution which went into effect in 1789. As such, the Bill of Rights are not amendable nor are they revocable. Also, the rights which were defined and established in the Constitution's first ten amendments apply to all citizens, regardless of race, color, or creed.

There is a growing effort by many of those in leadership positions in federal, state, and local governments to suppress rights when they are held by certain groups of people who elect to disagree with their views, agendas, and actions.

For example, the first amendment to the United States Constitution reads as follows:

Congress shall make no law respecting an establishment of religion, or prohibiting the free exercise thereof; or abridging the freedom of speech, or of the press; or the right of the people peaceably to assemble, and to petition the Government for a redress of grievances.

Numerous individuals and organizations over the years have tried and have to some extent succeeded in twisting the meaning of these words. When the First Amendment and its individual parts are examined, the following facts are established:

1. ***<u>Congress shall make no law respecting an establishment of religion.</u>***

    This means that the United States of America, unlike some other countries, does not utilize and may not establish a State Religion, or a religion whose practice is required by all citizens. Some people refer to this as the *Establishment Clause* which has been used by numerous secular groups such as American Atheists, Freedom from Religion, and other such organizations who have bullied, intimidated, and threatened schools, towns, cities, and municipalities which allow Christian symbols to be displayed on public property, in front of courthouses or other government buildings. Countless court cases and lawsuits consuming millions of dollars and countless hours of court time have been filed to threaten and force individuals, organizations, and municipalities to remove Christian symbols or monuments, some of which have stood with a community's admiration and respect for years. Families have even been threatened to remove memorials established on the side of roadways where loved ones have been tragically killed in accidents, despite the fact that those individuals and organizations making the complaint have nothing to do with and do not even personally know or have any regard for the people who they are threatening and what kind of tragedy their victims have already suffered and endured.

    On the contrary, the Establishment Clause protects the individual's religious freedom from government interference in both private as well as public sectors. The Establishment Clause does not create allowances for Congress to give one religion precedence over another, and it prohibits government interference with religious institutions for the purpose of furthering itself. In addition, the Establishment Clause DOES NOT prohibit the placement of religious monuments on government or other public buildings or property.

2.   *<u>or prohibiting the free exercise thereof</u>.*

Just as Congress can make no law establishing a State Religion, neither Congress nor any other organization, for that matter, may prohibit the free and open practice of an individual's religious faith in either public or private locations, nor may Congress, the courts, nor any other entity force a religious institution to condone or endorse a practice which is not in accordance with its beliefs. The practice and open expression of one's faith is also not restricted to a person's home or place of worship.

3.   *<u>or abridging the freedom of speech</u>.*

All rights come with responsibilities. The freedom of speech has been abused by many individuals and organizations over the years; however, the basic right of freedom of speech is applicable to all people, regardless of race, color, creed, or opinion.

In recent years, however, many legislative leaders at all levels of government have openly and intentionally tried to restrict the freedom of speech of those who disagree with their principles, opinions, and agendas.

In 2019, Brian Sims, a Pennsylvania state representative openly, publicly, and viciously verbally assaulted a woman and her teenage daughters (ages thirteen and fifteen) for peacefully praying outside a Planned Parenthood clinic. According to news reports, Sims initiated the confrontation, left the scene, then returned with a camera and began filming the woman, Ashley Garecht, and her two daughters while shouting at them and degrading them in public. Sims allegedly offered one hundred dollars to anyone who would reveal the identity of the two teenage girls, referred to Garecht as an "old white lady," and degraded her about her Christian beliefs: beliefs which are protected under the First Amendment of the United States Constitution.

4. ___or of the press___.

The press is responsible for the reporting unbiased facts relating to situations, events, and individuals or groups. The press does not have the right to promote opinions or ideologies supportive of one group or one opinion over another. Neither does the press possesses the right to publicly report nor publish information that may endanger private individuals, businesses, law enforcement officers, first responders, or military personnel. While the press has the right and responsibility to identify and report the truth, the press has often misused and abused that right. The freedom of the press is and must be limited by specific factors and situations which may be internal in nature, such as a code of ethics, or external in nature, such as public interest and safety, a ruling of a court, potential or possible libel actions, and so forth.

5. ___or the right of the people peaceably to assemble, and to petition the Government for a redress of grievances.___

An important thing to note here is the requirement which pertains to the right: Peaceful Assembly. A rioting mob which is engaged in violence and destruction of property does not constitute a peaceful assembly nor is a meeting where individuals are unruly, disrespectful, and who speak out of order. Many meetings which were convened for constructive purposes have disintegrated into uncontrolled arguments and fights.

Another critical issue involved in the ratification of the Constitution was the importance of preserving the right of law-abiding citizens to protect and defend themselves, their property, and their nation. The patriots who fought at the Battle of Lexington in 1775 were not armed with military-issued firearms. Instead, they were armed with their own personal weapons. Remembering the importance of this right, our Founding Fathers drafted and approved the Second Amendment to the Constitution: The Right to Keep and Bear Arms.

> _"A well-regulated Militia, being necessary to the security of a free State, the right of the people to keep and bear Arms, shall not be infringed."_

(Second Amendment to the United States Constitution.
Adopted on December 15, 1791.)

Like the First Amendment, the Second Amendment to the Constitution is under vicious attacks by socialist representatives and senators, not only in Washington, DC, but at state and local levels of government as well. A more in-depth look at socialism's attack on the Bill of Rights will be addressed in a later chapter.

America has faced many enemies, both near and far, throughout its history. Members of the United States Armed Forces take the following oath upon their enlistment to serve:

> *I, (Name), do solemnly swear (or affirm) that I will support and defend the Constitution of the United States against all enemies, foreign and domestic; that I will bear true faith and allegiance to the same; and that I will obey the orders of the President of the United States and the orders of the officers appointed over me, according to regulations and the Uniform Code of Military Justice. So help me God.*

Members of the United States government are required to take the following oath prior to entering office:

> *I do solemnly swear (or affirm) that I will support and defend the Constitution of the United States against all enemies, foreign and domestic; that I will bear true faith and allegiance to the same; that I take this obligation freely, without any mental reservation or purpose of evasion; and that I will well and faithfully discharge the duties of the office on which I am about to enter. So help me God.*

With members of the armed forces, the House of Representatives, the Senate, the president, and even members of the law enforcement community required to take an oath to support and defend the Constitution of the United States against all enemies, foreign and domestic, it would seem that this precious document would be held in high regard and reverence. But over the past several decades, due to the creeping tide of socialism, which continues to encroach upon the shores of American society, there has been an increasing effort to attack the Constitution, modify it, or even do away with it.

While United States Supreme Court Justice Sonia Sotomayor claims that the Constitution should not be bent under any circumstances, her counterpart, Ruth Bader Ginsburg, is alleged to have stated if she were drafting a constitution in 2012, she would not consider referring to the Constitution which was drafted by our Founding Fathers and ratified by the delegates of the original thirteen colonies. Over the years, an increasing number of legislators have expressed a desire to strip portions of the Constitution which serve as obstacles to their goals and agendas. This hostile aggression against the rights for which so many have served, fought, and died to protect is coupled with a growing complacency in American culture towards the seriousness of this threat.

As time marches steadily forward into the twenty-first century, and the promotion of socialism in American culture and politics continues, the future of those precious rights and freedoms provided for and guaranteed by the Constitution of the United States is becoming increasingly uncertain.

CHAPTER TWO

WHAT IS SOCIALISM?

According to the Merriam-Webster dictionary, Socialism is a term used to refer to various political and economic theories of government under which the ownership, administration, means of production, and distribution of goods is controlled solely by the government. Another factor of socialism is that, under its authority, there is no private ownership of property. There are a variety of views which fall under the umbrella of Socialism.

According to one view, under the economic system of socialism, everyone owns the various factors of production, and that ownership is obtained through the leadership of a democratically elected government. Under socialism, theoretically, everyone in society receives a share of the benefits of production. Socialism also allegedly advocates the more a person contributes to the economy, the larger the share of its profits they receive.

Some scholars imply the components of socialism and communism are interchangeable. While this is not completely accurate, it is a statement worthy of discussion. Socialism is one minor step below communism. Under socialism, the government exerts increasing control over the rights, opportunities, and freedoms of its citizens, while under communism, the government controls, monitors, and exerts authority over all aspects of an individual's life. Under Communism, the concept of freedom becomes only a distant memory. Kevin D. Williamson stated in his article: "The Politically Incorrect Guide to Socialism," "*The difference between Communism and Socialism is that under Socialism, central planning ENDS with a gun in your face, whereas under Communism, central planning BEGINS with a gun in your face.*" (Williamson, 2011)

The roots of socialism go far back in the span of human history. Ancient monarchies, the feudal system of the Middle Ages, and other cultures all displayed some elements of socialism.

During the Middle Ages, feudal lords owned and controlled the land and reaped its benefits while the peasants, with no real rights or benefits, labored for the good of their feudal masters hoping to receive protection from them against the many perils of that day and age. As time passed, some individuals began to envision the concept of an equal or classless society in which all people own everything, and everyone shares in the collective profit of a culture's labor. This ideology is the basis of what would become known as socialism. The foundation of modern socialism was conceived by Karl Marx and Friedrich Engels.

Karl Heinrich Marx was born in Prussia in 1818 in the city of Trier to a Jewish family of nine children. Marx's father, who was a lawyer, later converted to Lutheranism. As a child, Karl Marx was baptized as a Lutheran but later professed to be an atheist.

Marx's life was plagued by various problems. While attending the University of Bonn in Germany, Marx was arrested and imprisoned for being drunk in public and fighting a duel with another university student. Marx later enrolled in the University of Berlin, studying law and philosophy. It was while studying at the University of Berlin that Marx was introduced to the influence of university professor G.F.W. Hegel. Under Hegel's mentorship, Marx became a radical revolutionary and joined others under Hegel's influence in denouncing many institutions including politics, ethics, philosophy, and religious faith.

After receiving his degree from the University of Berlin, Marx was employed by the Rheinische Zeitung, a liberal democratic newspaper. In 1842, Marx became the paper's editor. It was during that period Marx married Jenny von Westphalen. The couple would have a total of seven children, of which only three would survive to reach adulthood.

As Marx's writings in the Rheinische Zeitung became more and more radical, his work caught the attention and aroused the concern of the Prussian government. In 1843, shortly after his marriage, Marx and his wife relocated to Paris, France. It was in Paris Marx met a German immigrant named Friedrich Engels who would become Marx's lifetime friend and supporter.

The concerns of the Prussian government followed Marx to France, and after the Prussian government began applying political pressure on the French leadership, Marx, his wife, and Engels moved to Brussels, Belgium. While in Belgium, Marx and Engels were hired by a newly formed organization known as the Communist League which was based in London, England. It was during this time Marx wrote his most well-known work, *The Communist Manifesto*, which he co-authored with Engels. The book was published in 1848.

Marx's writings also drew sharp criticism of the Belgium government, resulting in his departure from the country in 1848. After a short stay in Paris and Germany, Marx finally moved to England and settled in London. He was never awarded British citizenship and worked as a correspondent for the *New York Daily Tribune*. Never managing to earn even a meager living through any of his endeavors, Marx's family lived in poverty in London, and Marx received financial support from Engels for the better part of his life. He died of pleurisy on March 14, 1883.

In the Communist Manifesto, Marx and Engels describe what they conceive as a struggle between various economic classes in society and declare this struggle would eventually end with a violent overthrow of the capitalist form of economy and government. As an example, Marx cited the French Revolution, in which the wealthy and prominent upper class of France was overthrown and subjected to mass murder by the lower class. Marx implied that following this social upheaval, the proletariat (workers) would then assume control of the nation's means of production, and over time, the government would more-or-less cease to exist. In its wake, a classless society and economy would emerge which was based on common or mutual ownership of all the people practicing the following system of provision: *"from each according to his ability, to each according to his need."*

Marx identified various issues which he viewed as "evils" in his message of socialism, including the private ownership of property, the power of the wealthy, the loyalty of the family, authority of institutions of social control, and the influence of religion. Marx believed these factors of society were used to subjugate the working class and hinder them from receiving what was rightfully theirs. In response to the so-called oppression of the ruling class, Marx was an advocate of multiple means to bring his idea of rule into existence within a society. Those means included the use of violent force.

In his writings, Marx identified ten planks, or tenants, of Socialism. These include:

1. The abolishment of private property in land and application of all rents of land to public use.
2. A heavy progressive or graduated income tax.
3. Abolishment of all rights of inheritance.
4. The confiscation of the property of all emigrants and rebels.
5. The centralization of credit in the hands of the state by means of a national bank with state capital and an exclusive monopoly.
6. The centralization of the means of communication and transportation in the hands of the state.
7. The extension of factories and instruments of production owned by the state; the bringing into cultivation of waste lands, and the improvement of the soil generally in accordance with a common plan.
8. The equal obligation of all to work and the establishment of industrial armies, especially for agriculture.
9. The combination of agriculture with manufacturing industries; gradual abolishment of the distinction between town and country by a more equable distribution of the population over the country.
10. Free education for all children in government schools, and the abolishment of children's factory labor along with a combination of education with industrial production.

Socialism in various forms was already in existence a few decades before Marx published his famous work, and each had its own proponent who was convinced his form of socialism was the best. Some of these include Henri de Saint-Simon, whose followers desired and attempted to develop a utopian type society. Other include Robert Owen, Charles Fourier, Pierre Leroux, and Pierre-Joseph Proudhon.

The common denominator of these early socialist proponents were their ideas of equal distribution of wealth, solidarity among the working class, a desire for better working conditions, and the common ownership of productive resources, including land and equipment used in manufacturing. Although multiple experimental communities were established on the basic principles promoted by socialism's early proponents, none of these would survive the test of time.

The suffering of individuals throughout history has often served as a catalyst upon which tyranny is conceived. Leaders throughout history have attempted and successfully wooed untold thousands to their fold with the promises of equality, security, and prosperity. In many cases, the ordeal of suffering and hardship facing a culture's population has served to blind their eyes to the reality of what would-be dictators desire: total and absolute control.

Amid the diffuse collection of socialist ideologies which emerged in the eighteenth and nineteenth centuries, Karl Marx began attacking these insufficient and flawed ideas of socialism with his own brand, which Engels referred to as scientific socialism. Marx proposed that many deeply rooted norms in society must be uprooted and prohibited if true equality and social justice were to take hold and survive.

To a socialist, all that exists and is relevant is the material world and suffering in the material world is the result of an unequal distribution of wealth. Marx implied in his message of socialism that one of the oppressors of a suffering society was Faith and Religion.

Faith in a Superior Being (God) has been a part of man's history since he first appeared on the earth. In his efforts to displace faith and religion with humanism and socialism, Marx invented the concept of what he referred to as the notion of dielectric materialism.

Dielectric Materialism is a belief that matter contains a creative power within itself; therefore, there is no need for a Creator or the belief in a creator or any such Supreme Being. In the concept of religion, salvation comes through faith, while in the concept of socialism conceived by Marx, salvation is sought and achieved only through the redistribution of wealth, and spirituality has no place in a just and equal society. Marx assumed and preached that if everyone has the same amount of material possessions, all the problems and struggles in a society, culture, or nation will cease to exist. It is interesting to note that Karl Marx accepted assistance and support from others throughout his life but was a failure in providing the basic needs for his wife and children.

While socialism has become a common term, its exact definition is not very distinctive. There are multiple views and definitions of what socialism truly is depending on who is providing the definition. If you speak to ten different individuals who are proponents of socialism, you will probably get ten different definitions and statements on what socialism is and what it promotes.

CHAPTER THREE

THE HISTORY OF SOCIALISM

Socialism's initial appearance in human culture probably began as a response to the severe and often inhumane working conditions which plagued the industrialized society of European nations in early part of the nineteenth century. Robert Owen, mentioned earlier, was a Welsh mill owner in the 1820s who developed "utopian" communities based on the general provisions of socialism. None of the utopian communities envisioned or established by Owen or others who shared his ideologies survived for long.

The writings of Karl Marx fanned the flames for the growth of socialism in the nineteenth and twentieth centuries. Scholar Paul Brians, in a summary of socialists' thinking stated, *"Socialist rejected the argument that the wealthy deserve their wealth because they created it, instead believing that wealth is created by the working class and wrongly appropriated by the rich."* (Brians, 2016)

The growing tensions in a world racked by wars, social injustices, economic troubles, various crises, and political unrest provided fertile grounds for sowing the seeds of socialism and enabling them to sprout from the soil of calamity. One of the earliest events of the twentieth century which led to the establishment of socialism, which later morphed into communism, was the Bolshevik Revolution of October 1917.

The tumultuous hardships of the First World War weighed heavily on the people of Russia. Tsar Nicholas II, the last of the Romanov rulers, reigned as head of state of a nation which was literally falling apart. Shortages of food caused riots to break out among the starving population. Disgruntled civilians were soon joined by disgruntled soldiers. Desertion in the Russian army was rampant, and the Russian military began to lose its efficiency as a fighting force.

In addition, due to the Russian army being poorly equipped and led by seemingly incompetent leadership, the Russian military suffered disastrous losses in the bitter fighting taking place on the Eastern Front. The inability of the Russian military to hold its own in combat led many to fear it could not defend the homeland with any hope of victory. Also, government corruption and the abhorrent financial cost of the war plunged Russia's economy into utter chaos. Lured by the offers of food, peace, and other promises, the hungry peasants of Russian citizenry, along with thousands of angry soldiers and sailors, flocked to the revolutionary cause.

Unable to hold his throne, Tsar Nicholas II was forced to abdicate in March of 1915 after most of the Russian infantry composing the garrison at St. Petersburg had joined the general population in the growing revolt against him. Nicholas's brother, Grand Duke Michael, refused to take the throne, and the Romanov Dynasty which had stood for over three hundred years finally came to an end. Eventually, Tsar Nicholas II, along with his family, were executed in July of 1918.

In the aftermath of the October Revolution, conflict between the competing factions plunged Russia into a two-year civil war, from which the Bolsheviks emerged victorious. The socialist ideologies which had fueled the revolution in turn gave way to the emergence of an even more severe system of government: communism.

Another event that sowed the seeds for the cultivation of a socialist government was the Treaty of Versailles which ended World War I. The treaty, signed on June 28, 1919, levied extremely harsh retributions upon the nation of Germany, and was drafted solely by the allied powers without any input allowed by German representatives.

In accordance with the Treaty of Versailles, Germany was forced to cede large amounts of territory, including Eupen-Malmedy, Alsace-Lorraine, various Eastern Districts, Memel, and large areas of Schleswig to Belgium, France, Poland, Lithuania, and Denmark, respectively. In addition, Germany was forced to give up control over all its colonies. Along with the loss of territory, Germany was forced to pay extremely costly financial reparations to Allied powers for damages and cost of the war. However, one of the most humiliating aspects of the treaty for Germany was its impact on the nation's military.

Under the Treaty of Versailles, Germany's military was reduced to little more than a national security force with limited numbers of troops, extreme limitations on the number and size of naval vessels, as well as the prohibition of certain types of ships including submarines, aircraft carriers, and capital ships displacing over ten thousand tons. The treaty left Germany in a basically defenseless condition, and while the German government signed the Treaty of Versailles under protest, many German leaders and military officers acted in defiance of what they felt were unjust actions imposed by the treaty. In Scapa Flow, the main British naval base in Scotland, the German commander gave an order to scuttle the German warships which had been interned there by the British government.

In the wake of the Treaty of Versailles, Germany was plunged into political and economic chaos. Large scale unemployment, runaway inflation, and national humiliation began to fester like an infected wound, laying the groundwork for the emergence of a government which would wreak havoc among war weary nations and ignite the flames of yet another global conflict. It is ironic that the coming revolution and subsequent conflict which was to follow was literally born out of the ambitions of a single individual.

On April 20, 1889 in a small town near the Austro-German frontier, a couple saw the birth of a son who, unbeknownst to them, would launch the world into a war which would last over six years, result in catastrophic collateral damage to uncountable cities, and result in the deaths of over sixty million people. His name was Adolf Hitler.

Following the deaths of his father in 1903 and his mother in 1908, Hitler struggled to make his way in the turbulent years leading up to World War I. He was not a good student and dropped out of secondary school. He moved to Vienna following the death of his mother with a strong desire to become an artist but was rejected by the Vienna Academy of Fine Arts. Working on his own, he struggled to make a living painting and selling his works amongst a disinterested Venetian population.

Discouraged and increasingly angry, Adolf Hitler moved to Munich, Germany in 1913 and settled in the region of Bavaria. The First World War erupted the following year, and Hitler found a new home in the German army. He served as a messenger and eventually rose to the rank of corporal.

During the first Battle of the Somme in 1916, Hitler was wounded in the leg. Later, in the fighting near Ypres in 1918, he was temporarily blinded by poison gas. While he was recovering in a hospital near Berlin, Hitler was informed of the Armistice between the Central and Allied powers and was depressed to learn of his nation's defeat. In the aftermath of the war, Hitler, along with many other Germans, began to conceive the idea that the blame for Germany's humiliating defeat lay at the feet the German leadership itself.

After his recovery, Hitler moved to Munich and became part of a small political party known as the German Workers' Party. The German Workers' Party longed to revive a sense of German national pride and unite the suffering working class against the German leadership which the party viewed as corrupt, unreliable, and untrustworthy.

While lacking any higher education, Hitler proved himself to be gifted with excellent speaking skills and the ability to seize the attention of his audience. This talent enabled him to move rapidly through the ranks of the German Worker's Party. As his role of leadership grew, he was able to give the party a new name: The National Socialist German Workers Party (i.e. Nazi Party) which adopted the swastika as its emblem.

Between the years of 1918 and 1921, the Nazi Party continued to grow in numbers largely due to Hitler's persuasive speeches and propaganda. Through speeches, written notices, and other means, the Nazi Party began to ramp up its efforts to spread discontent and distrust in the Weimar Republic of Germany and angrily denounced the harsh terms of the Treaty of Versailles, which the Nazi Party implied was to blame for the current state of Germany's social-economic condition. A large number of disgruntled army officers, including Ernst Rohm, would flock to the ranks of the Nazi Party. Rohm would later be responsible for recruiting protection squads referred to as the Sturmabteilung (SA). The SA was used by Hitler to provide security for Nazi Party meetings and to openly attack any opponents of their cause.

The situation boiled over on November 8, 1923, when Hitler, members of the SA, and other party supporters entered a tavern where a right-wing opponent was speaking to the tavern's occupants. Hitler produced a pistol, proclaimed the Nazi Party was taking control of the German government, and led a large mob to the center of the city of Munich where a gunfight with the German police ensued. Hitler's ploy failed, and he was arrested, tried for treason, and sentenced to five years imprisonment in Landsberg Castle.

After serving nine months of his sentence, Hitler was released from prison and renewed his efforts to woo the nation of Germany to the fold of the Nazi Party. In his book *Mein Kampf* (My Struggle), which was written during his incarceration, Hitler outlined his plan for the rebound of Germany from the depths of despair caused by the Treaty of Versailles and the inefficiency of the Weimar Republic. Over the years, Hitler's book has become a best seller, second only to the Holy Bible. Hitler established a new version of the SA known as the Schutzstaffel (SS), who swore an oath of personal loyalty to Hitler and became the terror of Europe in the years following its conception.

Following an intense campaign of propaganda and the failure of three successive German rulers to maintain control of the country which was now locked in the embrace of the Great Depression which began in 1929, Hitler was able to finally make his move to power. In 1933, the aged President Paul von Hindenburg proclaimed Adolf Hitler as Chancellor of Germany. Following a devastating fire at Germany's Parliament building, the Reichstag, Hitler was able to successfully persuade the German Parliament to pass the Enabling Act in 1933 which gave him full autocratic power. In July of that same year, the Nazi Party became the only recognized political party in Germany and all other political, industrial, and civic organizations not associated with the Nazis were abolished.

While Hitler's success seemed to be increasing, there were dissidents within the ranks of his own party who potentially composed an obstacle to his future endeavors. On June 29, 1934, The Night of the Long Knives, Hitler's forces murdered hundreds of potential troublemakers. Hindenburg died on August 2nd of that year, and the German military leadership agreed to combine the German presidency and Chancellorship into a single office. All opposition, verbal, written, or otherwise, was violently prohibited, and the freedom of speech and choice were trampled underfoot by the unnerving march of Nazi boots.

As his grip on power increased, Hitler cast aside the restrictions of the Treaty of Versailles and began rebuilding Germany's devastated military. Between 1936 and 1938, German troops under Hitler's orders marched into Austria, the left bank of the Rhine River, and Czechoslovakia. Out of fear of being pulled into another armed conflict neither England, France, nor the rest of the world responded to Hitler's military aggression. By the time the former allied powers finally made the decision to act, it was too late. German troops invaded

Poland in September of 1939, and the Second World War became a sad reality. It would take six years of warfare and millions of casualties from many nations to bring Hitler's Nazi Third Reich to a fiery and catastrophic end.

But the problems did not stop there. The Russians, communist relatives of the Nazi German Socialists, helped bring about Hitler's demise from the East while the remainder of the Allied forces assailed him from the West. But the Russians had their own post-war goals in mind which would bring about a new and strange conflict which later became known as the Cold War.

In a sense, the road to the expansion of socialism and its successor, communism, was paved before the end of the Second World War. Some of the tools employed by socialist proponents in the construction of their regimes include propaganda, censorship, and authoritative control.

Both socialist and communist deception involves the initial persuasion of a population to cede control of the control and distribution of goods and services to the state with the promise of equality and prosperity in return. Another deception of the socialist agenda involves the implication that the workers own the means of production and therefore cannot be exploited by any ruling class or other entity. However, this concept was merely a ploy to win people's trust until the socialist leaders and supporters were firmly in control. It is in the aftermath of a socialist takeover that the true ugliness of such regimes becomes truly apparent.

As the Russian army advanced westward toward Germany, one of their first actions when gaining a foothold in a new territory was to take over any local radio stations and use them to spread propaganda praising their system, efforts, and accomplishments while condemning and denouncing the ideologies of their opponents. Many people in Soviet occupied regions fell victim to the words of promise and justice proclaimed by the advancing Russian forces. As socialist/communist forces gained control over a region, they would in turn recruit security forces to protect and defend their agenda. Little by little, the civil population of first a region and then a nation would hand over more and more of their freedoms in exchange for the expected return of the promise of equality and prosperity offered by their socialist/communist overlords. In the end, the people's freedom was gone, and socialist/communist leadership was firmly in control before anyone realized what was happening.

One of the key elements of Soviet-promoted socialist/communist governments was the goal of the security of the Soviet Union itself. After the hardships and tragedies suffered by the Russian people during the invasion and occupation of large regions of the country by the armed forces of Nazi Germany, the Soviet leadership wanted to defend itself against any repeat of Hitler's failed plan to topple the Soviet regime. To accomplish this task, the Russian leadership endeavored to create a buffer zone between the East and the West.

The populations of the countries of Eastern Europe suffered greatly during the Second World War. Caught between Nazi Germany on one side and Russia on the other, they were often forced to take one side or the other to find the least painful solution to their situation. Finland, a nation which fought desperately for its survival during the Winter War of 1939/1940 against Russia, finding no other source of support, was forced to seek assistance from Germany in order to maintain its fight against Russian military aggression. In return, many Finns were forced to serve in Waffen SS units of the German army in its own campaign against the Soviets. In addition, many of these countries possessed valuable natural resources which were desperately desired and sought after by both sides.

Romanian oil was critical to the Nazi war effort. Hungary, Austria, and Czechoslovakia provided roads for that oil to be routed to Germany. Austria and Hungary provided routes into Yugoslavia which in turn provided access to the Mediterranean Sea, which was a lifeline to the German troops fighting in Africa. Bulgaria provided a barrier against invasion from the southeast, and Poland provided valuable ports for the imports of Swedish iron ore.

But just as the Eastern European nations provided a value to the efforts of Nazi Germany, they later provided a value to the advancement of socialism and communism. As Russian forces moved westward, taking over one territory after another, the Soviet leadership was in no hurry to withdraw them after the armistice and cessation of hostilities.

At the end of the War in Europe in 1945, General George Patton openly expressed his concerns over the continued Soviet presence in Eastern Europe. With the Third Army under his command, Patton's troops were standing by on the outskirts of Prague in Czechoslovakia. Across from the Third Army waited the Soviet Army which was under overall command of Soviet Field Marshal Georgy Zhukov. General Patton urgently requested that General Dwight Eisenhower, the overall Allied Commander in Chief, permit his forces to engage and drive back the Russian forces. He was supported by British Prime Minister Sir Winston Churchill who also recognized the threat posed by continued Soviet occupation in Eastern Europe. However, their pleas fell on deaf ears.

In the ensuing months, communist forces gained control of Czechoslovakia, Berlin, and other regions in the East. In time, Eastern Germany, Poland, Lithuania, Estonia, Romania, Bulgaria, Hungary, Austria, Yugoslavia, and other countries were firmly under the yoke and influence of socialist or communist governments. After being defeated in his bid for re-election as prime minister in 1945, Churchill was invited to Westminster College in Fulton, Missouri in 1946, where he delivered his famous speech denouncing Soviet policies and actions in post-war Europe, and in which he made his famous statement, *"From Stettin in the Baltic to Trieste in the Adriatic, an iron curtain has descended across the continent."* (Churchill, 1946)

As the grip of socialism and communism gained a stronghold over Eastern Europe and began to spread into Southeast Asia, many people who had fallen victim to socialism's deception began to realize the harsh reality of socialist/communist control over their lives. What little freedoms they knew were lost, their right to speak out against their government's totalitarian oppression was silenced, and countless people were victimized, families were separated, opponents were suppressed, and dissidents were imprisoned or killed all in the name of socialism and communism. The promise of the people being in control faded into the shadow of totalitarian governmental control, and large expanses of the European continent descended into another Dark Ages.

In time, the seeds of socialism were flung across the entire world, coming to rest on numerous and, at times, unsuspecting societies. Some of those seeds would in time come to rest in a nation which was founded as a democracy: The United States of America.

Chapter Four

The Flaws of Socialism

Socialism has never existed in pure form in any country on Earth, neither has it been constructively employed nor utilized as an effective form of government anywhere it has been tried. The reasons for socialism's failure lie in its many flaws. Some scholars have suggested that socialism will never succeed anywhere in human culture.

According to Mark J. Perry, professor of economics and finance at the University of Michigan, "*Socialism will always fail because it's a flawed system based on completely faulty principles that aren't consistent with human behavior and can't nurture the human species.*" Perry went on to suggest, "*Socialism is the big lie of the twentieth century. While it promised prosperity, equality, and security, it delivered poverty, misery, and tyranny.*" (Perry, 1995)

One of the biggest elements contributing to the failure of the system of socialism is the fact that it disregards the importance of incentives. The centrality of a nation's economics under socialism does not encourage an individual to work hard and strive for excellence. The proponents of socialism typically have no interest in the well-being of the general population. Rather, the primary goal of the proponents of Socialism is the establishment of totalitarian control to force their agenda on people whether they agree with that agenda or not. Socialism's common enticement is to persuade a population to give up a portion its freedom in return for more security; however, in the end both freedom and security are eventually lost.

Benjamin Franklin once made the statement: *"Those who would trade the essential freedoms for temporary safety deserve neither and lose both."* While this conclusion may seem a bit rash, it has been repeatedly proven as true wherever socialism has gained a foothold over a group of people. On many occasions, it is more likely a population was drawn into the web of the socialist spider before recognizing the trap into which it was about to fall.

One of the first flaws of socialism lies in the fact that it suppresses the value of the very first established institution in human culture: Marriage and Family. A key target of socialism is young people who are easily enticed and deceived. Socialism endeavors to replace the family with the State, so the State can indoctrinate children according to socialist ideology. Friedrich Engel, co-author of the *Communist Manifesto*, once stated that the society which he sought to create would be one in which the single-family unit no longer exists, private housekeeping would be transformed into a social industry, and the care and education of children would be a public matter.

The collapse of the single-family unit in American society is becoming a cultural collapse of America itself. Children grow up in situation where they have no mother, no father, or in some cases, neither parent present in their lives. The stability of the home is compromised by an increasing secular human ideology which is infecting the American society to an ever-increasing degree each day. Traditional and long-established families beginning with a husband and a wife are under increasing attack by proponents of socialism, and American culture is hanging by a thread over the edge of a proverbial cliff awaiting the moment of disaster. Before there were governments, constitutions, monarchies, city states, or even simple villages, there was the family. If the traditional family, which composes the foundation of a society, ceases to exist, it will only be a matter of time before the society itself collapses into chaos.

A second reason socialism cannot succeed is that it ignores the basic human attribute of Faith in a Higher Power. While, socialism tends to tolerate certain religious groups and practices, it adamantly openly opposes the Christian Faith or any faith which holds beliefs contrary to the views of socialism.

Karl Marx envisioned a society which had no place for a "creator." While the Bible teaches that suffering is often the result of sin or disobedience to the Word of God, Marx implied that suffering was caused by the unequal distribution of the wealth within a society, and salvation was obtained through the redistribution of that wealth. As mentioned earlier, Marx believed if everyone had the same amount of material possessions that all problems within a society would eventually cease to exist.

Marxism envisions only a material world in which no issues of a spiritual nature exist. However, the spiritual nature of mankind has been recognized and accepted form the beginning of history. Robert W. Faid, a nuclear engineer, stated in his book *A Scientific Approach to Christianity*, that Neanderthal Man buried his dead with tools, food, and so forth indicating the belief in an afterlife.

Socialism also attacks the concept of virtue, which is instilled within human beings by their faith. Life teaches mankind that there are rewards and consequences for one's actions. While there are many definitions of success, its reality stems from hard work, commitment, and a desire to achieve excellence. Labor brings reward, while a refusal to work leads to need.

Socialism believes in rewarding all people whether they deserve it or not. While some individuals are not able to support themselves due to handicaps, illness, or injury, there are many people today who believe in receiving a free handout without taking any action to improve their situation. Panhandlers are often observed standing on the sides of roadways around the nation for hours at a time holding signs decrying their desperate need but later walk two or three blocks to a perfectly fine automobile and drive home to an equally fine house.

Socialism's concept of the redistribution of wealth promotes the taking of material possessions and wealth from one person and giving it to another, regardless of the reality or nonreality of a need, or whether the receiving individual has made any effort to improve their individual situation or not. In a sense, Socialism erases the need or desire for an individual to have motivations and incentives to improve their situation. Incentives are a driving factor in a growing economy. The desire and ambition to produce a better product or service and to deliver that product or service with the utmost efficiency in expectation of the reward of material gain in return are very productive. The idea of receiving a reward in return for good and productive work ethics has made paupers into millionaires.

At the age of thirteen, a young boy named George who worked at his father's machine shop in Schenectady, New York, was once obsessed with keeping a meeting with some of his friends in regards to a bet he had made with them over a small engine he had built for a boat. After finding out his father had plans for him to work in the shop cutting pipes on the same day he was to keep his engagement with his friends, George quickly invented and assembled a machine which automatically loaded and cut the pipes, allowing him to be in two places at the same time. George Westinghouse Jr. would go on to discover alternating current, develop the air brake, and countless other inventions which propelled him from the small machine shop to the head of a corporation. His rewards were not a gift but rather the fruits of his labor.

Another interesting and inspiring example of the achievements of hard work and dedicated work ethics may be seen in the life of a man who grew up in poverty in Houston, Texas. His name was Paul Neil Adair.

Paul, otherwise known as "Red," Adair, was forced to drop out of high school after the death of his parents. He worked at numerous manual labor jobs but had a burning desire to get into the oil business. His will and tenacious efforts eventually got him a job with a company called Otis Pressure Control.

It was while working with Otis Pressure Control that Adair's abilities, which would lead to his future successes, would come to light. While working on a gas well near Smackover, Arkansas, Adair found himself face to face with one of the most terrifying industrial situations: a gas well blowout. The well which Adair and the crew he was assigned to were working on suddenly began to exhibit a violent upsurge of pressure, and in an instant, high-pressure natural gas was blasting through the well head valve assembly at thousands of psi.

The work crew ran for their lives; all except Adair who, after taking a moment to inspect the problem, identified a loose component on the valve assembly. He rushed to the company work truck and retrieved the necessary tools which he had cleaned and stowed the night before. In a matter of minutes, Adair had brought the potential disaster back under control.

His achievements that day would eventually lead to his working with another daredevil: Myron Kinley. Under Kinley's mentorship, Adair was introduced to the exciting and extremely dangerous field of fighting oil well fires and controlling oil and gas well blowouts. As time went by, Adair became the world's leading expert in his field and went from a poverty-stricken high school dropout to a multimillionaire, not through a constant, subsidized handout, but through a sincere dedication to doing a job to the best of his ability and constantly striving to make himself better. But socialism has a different view on life.

Socialism tends to punish individuals who are industrious and hardworking by insisting they provide sustenance, material, and financial support for individuals who do not desire to be industrious and hard working. Socialist ideology even advocates the taking of property and wealth from one person and giving it to another regardless of whether a person truly needs help or assistance, or if they are deserving such assistance. In addition, socialism seeks to abolish the personal ownership of property. Even the Bible, the Tenth Commandment warns mankind not to covet or desire what belongs to another and acknowledges a person's right to own their own property. According to some economic scholars, the right to own property coupled with market force price determination and a profit-and-loss system of accounting are the strengths of capitalist-type economies which are found to work successfully in nations around the world today.

Another flaw in socialism is its assumption that human beings are always completely cooperative in their efforts. If human beings were so cooperative, there would be no conflicts anywhere in the world today. While nations in the past have endeavored to work together in the face of a common crisis, that cooperation has never been without some internal conflict and crippling disagreements.

During the Second World War, Great Britain became an uneasy ally of Russian, not because of any agreement with nor support of the concept of communism, but because both nations were faced with the prospect of annihilation by a common enemy. As an ancient proverb dating back almost four thousand years BC states: *The enemy of my enemy is my friend*, even if the friend is one who merits keeping a wary eye on. The stubborn resistance of the Russian forces on the Eastern Front forced Germany to send vast quantities of troops, supplies, and equipment to that theatre of war; troops and equipment which could have be used against Great Britain, and Great Britain's naval forces were instrumental in ensuring that life-sustaining supplies were able to reach Russia's beleaguered military forces and desperate civilians.

The United States entered an initial alliance with Great Britain before America itself was drawn into the war by pledging material support and, eventually, the transfer of fifty World War I era destroyers to reinforce Britain's desperate navy which was struggling to counter the German offensive in the Atlantic. While hoping to avoid being drawn into the war itself, America knew the danger of allowing the influence and aggression of Nazi Germany to spread beyond the European theatre.

However, despite their open cooperation, there were continual and sometimes disruptive disagreements between the allies. Their top commanders often competed with one another instead of working as a team. One of the most disastrous of these competitions came to light due to Britain's desire to have an English military leader successfully complete a daring offensive in the wake of General George Patton's rousing success with the Third Army's in its onslaught against the German forces in the South. The military offensive proposed by British Field Marshall Montgomery was code named: Market Garden.

Operation Market Garden called for a charge into Holland in an all-out effort to reach the Bridge over the Rhine River at Arnhem, Holland. The plan consisted of a massive airborne assault of one British and two American airborne divisions, with the British units being accompanied by a Polish airborne brigade, along with the British 30th corps mobile infantry and armored division.

While the plan was a bold one, it was wracked with flaws and hindering variables. The entire airborne assault would take three days due to a shortage of aircraft, the single road which the British ground forces were forced to use was a prime target for German defenders, and each bridge along the way was critical to the success of the operation. In the end, the destruction of one bridge by artillery fire placed the advancing ground forces nearly two days behind schedule. Heavy German resistance at the Bridge located at the Dutch city of Nijmegen delayed the operation even further, and the rejection of critical intelligence by senior British officers led to their own airborne troops being dropped into the deadly midst of two German SS Panzer Divisions. The outcome was disastrous. Allied forces suffered an estimated seventeen thousand-plus casualties in the operation and failed to capture the critical bridge at Arnhem.

It is almost ironic that allied forces suffered more casualties during Operation Market Garden in 1945 than at the invasion of Normandy on D-Day! It is also tragic but obvious that factors leading to this tragedy included a failure on Britain's part to acknowledge and inform their American allies of the presence of German armored units at Arnhem, and well as the true strength of the German resistance. Operation Market Garden stands as a horrific example that most the cooperative efforts of humanity are still wracked with flaws.

From another perspective among the competing allied leaders, Russia was openly dissatisfied with the time it took to open the second front in Europe, and when the pressure on the Eastern Front was somewhat relieved, the communist forces exploited their opportunity to conquer and gain influence over as much territory as possible.

True complete and flawless cooperation within a society is almost impossible to achieve due to the instinctive desire of the individual to succeed and/or survive according to their own terms and ambitions. Individuals, groups, and so forth will cooperate to an extent in order to achieve their individual goals. However, once an individual's personal goals, desires, and initiatives are threatened their cooperation tends to disappear in support of a personal concerns.

One of the reasons that socialism and communism consistently fail lies in the hypocrisy of their proponents. In Soviet Russia, the people eventually discovered there existed a class within their "classless" society, and the proposed power of the people is little more than a shadowy mirage in the desert of the reality of the power of the government. Examples from around the world and throughout history show that the power of the government in the vast majority of socialist/communist regimes is typically supported by specific military units who are specially rewarded and provided for in return for their loyalty and protection.

A final and very concerning flaw of socialism is its path to absolute power. The Founding Fathers of America, in their endeavor to create a government of the people, by the people, and for the people, designed a structure of the government which would establish a system of checks and balances. Power is divided between three branches of government, and the actions and power of each branch of government is checked by the others preventing the establishment of absolute power. Or at least that is the way the system is supposed to work. Ultimate success or failure lies with the integrity of each branch to do its job without compromise of its duties and responsibilities.

While no government envisioned and established by mankind will ever be perfect, the government structure of the United States of America as set forth in its Constitution stands as one of the most effective and least oppressive in the world. Only the impact of human corruption, greed, immorality, and jealousy stains the government of the United States. According to Lord Acton, *"Power tends to corrupt and absolute power corrupts completely."* (Lord Acton, 1887)

Acton both boldly and correctly implies that any system of government without a system of checks and balances erases the existence of freedom and opens the door to oppression. For socialism to exist, even in corrupted forms, it demands an element of blind trust and faith in the individuals who hold the power to determine the overall well-being of the population. Human history has shown again and again that those who win the trust of the general population to hold that power tend to abuse it, and such abuse is often manifested in a tragic, unjust, and horrific manner.

CHAPTER FIVE

THE IMPACT OF SOCIALISM

Socialism is sold to a population with many promises and assurances, the majority of which are never delivered. People in desperate situations are at times easily persuaded to accept the empty promises offered by socialist proponents in the hopes of a better life for themselves and their families. Socialist leaders often make a show of standing and walking in the midst of the people who they desire to lure under their yoke in a show of concern and solidarity; however, it is usually a gimmick used to trick a population into blindly following their leadership.

Poverty has plagued societies for centuries. In the early 1800s, it has been estimated that over ninety percent of the global population lived in conditions that constituted poverty. Barely a century and a half later, that percentage had been roughly cut in half, and by the early twentieth century, the number of people living in poverty around the world was reduced to below twenty percent. But it was not socialism that made such a difference in lifting over one billion individuals from the depths of poverty; rather, it was the dynamics of capitalism and the foundations of freedom and human values.

The Russian mathematician Igor Shafarevich in his book *The Socialist Phenomenon*, presented multiple descriptions of how the impact of socialism ultimately leads to the suppression of such important matters such as freedom and individuality. Shafarevich stated there were certain components which are required for any long-term existence of a socialist-inspired culture and economic model. These components include: the elimination of the private ownership of private property, the dissolution or abolishment of the family unit, and convincing the population to focus on the idea of prosperity being centered around material possessions.

In time, the reality of socialism becomes apparent to those who have been subjected by it; however, by the time a nation realizes what it has lost, it is typically too late. As a nation plunges into the grip of socialism and its eventual spawn, communism, the people will, either willingly or unwillingly, and slowly but surely, hand over control of production, management of the distribution of resources, and the responsibility for security and protection, giving the state an ever-increasing control over the personal lives of its subjects.

As the power of a socialist government grows, its leaders will set in place a system of regulations which hinder or prohibit any dissent voiced against it by the people and establish an organization of armed enforcement to keep any of those who would dare speak out against the government's actions in check. The message of equality and unity makes an inspiring sermon from the socialist pulpit, but as such a government becomes well secured and in power, equality is thrown out the proverbial window in the name of national and social pacification. In time, the government will assume total control of all aspects of production, including food, housing, communication, education, medicine, transportation, and other areas. The socialist bureaucracy then distributes those resources as it sees fit to those who are the most loyal, supportive, and obedient. In the end, socialism delivers the exact opposite of what it promises.

In addition, the government also ends up in control of the media and the revelation of information relating to the events occurring in society, the status of the nation, and the needs of the people. A socialist-controlled media is heavily censored and only what the government wants the people to know is relayed to the general population, and with the censorship of the media and other means of communication comes the stark reality of intense government surveillance of its citizens.

A socialist or communist state often views its own people with suspicion, especially those who express discontent with the quality of their lives and the leadership qualities of their government. Along with the constant monitoring of the civil population by government security agencies, a system of travel restrictions within the nation itself may be instituted.

In Soviet Russia, citizens who were supposed to be equal and in control of the government found themselves trapped within their own cities and regions and could only travel from one part of the country to another with a government permit and their internal passport, unless, of course, they were part of the bureaucratic elite.

Socialism is promoted on the grounds it promises it will build up, unify, provide for, protect, and bring equality to a society. In the modern world, where everyone looks for the miracle cure for every problem from back pain to emotional instability, socialism implies that, under its wings, those who deserve better can have better by the redistribution of the achievements of others, and many individuals fall for the deception. However, in the end, the promise is revealed to be empty, and socialism ultimately destroys a society in multiple ways.

Socialism hinders and eventually wrecks economic growth. The existence of a thriving economy is essential to a nation's job growth, revenue, and standard of living. A strong economy, based on the constructive efforts of the population, benefits everyone. President John F. Kennedy once implied the rising tide of an economy lifts all boats.

By punishing successful workers and business leaders while providing a free handout to those who fail due to complacency, mismanagement, or just plain laziness, socialism cripples and eventually destroys the economic development of a nation over a period of time. When those who strive to be successful are punished by the State in that the fruits of their labor are stripped away and given to those who stand idly by and expect their sustenance to be provided for them,   both social and economic collapse is only a matter of time. The end result is that individuals become discouraged from being successful and encouraged to fail. As the drive to succeed is absorbed by the desire to receive government aid, the number of individuals who strive for success decreases, and the number of people who endeavor to fail grows.

As this trend progresses, a nation's economic wealth is eventually concentrated in the hands of a small number of leaders and the growth or development of an economy stagnates as more and more people come to depend and rely on government support. Eventually, an economy will slow to the point where it cannot produce enough revenue from taxation to sustain or support any of those in need, or who literally place themselves in need. The final harsh and tragic outcome eventually comes to light and the nation's economy collapses.

As the Founding Fathers of the United States of America struggled to complete a final draft of a constitution which would be approved of and ratified by all colonial delegates, they realized certain freedoms and rights must be clearly defined and protected. In the First Amendment to the United States Constitution, a very important freedom and right was defended and protected: the right to freedom of speech.

The history of man's desire for freedom of speech goes back to the Greek philosopher Socrates in 399 BC, when at his trial he defied the jury's demands that he keep silent rather than voice his disagreements with their accusations.

Problems within an individual, a family, an organization or business, or a society cannot be addressed and solved unless they are openly acknowledged and affirmed, whether it is a popular thing to acknowledge that such problems exist or not.

One of the nations in which the restrictions of freedom of speech were readily apparent was the former Soviet Union. In 1962, Russian writer Aleksandr Solzhenitsyn wrote a book entitled *One Day in the Life of Ivan Denisovich* in which he presented the stark conditions of a Soviet labor camp during the time of Joseph Stalin's rule in Russia. After twelve years of harsh criticism and rebuke, Solzhenitsyn was exiled from Russia in 1974. The suppression of freedom to speak out and identify problems and concerns not only infringes on the basic human desires to call attention to injustices, but can and has led to disasters in the past.

In September of 1986, a Soviet Navaga Class ballistic missile submarine, K-219, was preparing to depart on a regularly scheduled strategic deterrence patrol in the Atlantic Ocean. While inspecting the vessel in preparation for its upcoming departure, the ship's missile officer, Captain Third Rank Alexander Petrachkov, made an alarming discovery. The missile hatch for silo number six indicated a minor leak from the hatch ring, but while this was a serious material deficiency, Captain Third Rank Petrachkov was hesitant to report the problem to the ship's commanding officer, Captain Second Rank Igor Anatolyevich Britanov. Such a report could have possibly led to the vessel failing to depart for its mission on schedule, and such delays were often viewed with disfavor by the higher authorities of communist leadership. The failure to accomplish the State's objectives often led to unpleasant consequences for those individuals who caused such delays.

Rather than draw the unwanted attention and potentially severe repercussions on himself, his captain, and the rest of the crew that speaking out on this issue would surely bring, the ship's missile officer elected to keep quiet about the problem and directed his men to keep a close eye on the water level in missile silo six and pump the tube each watch rotation. K-219 departed its home port of Gadzhiyevo on its patrol on September 4, 1986 and proceeded to its patrol area in the Atlantic Ocean.

On October 3rd, approximately twenty-nine days into the submarine's patrol, a disaster of unprecedented proportions occurred. The slow leak from the hatch ring of silo number six suddenly erupted into a powerful inrush of seawater causing the missile tube to flood rapidly. To make matters worse, the R-27U ballistic missile in silo number six developed a fuel leak at the same time, spilling highly volatile nitrogen tetroxide into the tube. Due to the unfortunate fact that nitrogen tetroxide, an oxidizer, reacts explosively when mixed with sea water, the end result was inevitable.

As Petrachkov directed emergency actions to pump the tube, the seawater and rocket fuel mixture reached a critical point, and silo number six erupted in a cataclysmic explosion, blowing a hole through the upper part of the pressure hull of the submarine. Petrachkov and two missile technicians were killed instantly. Under Captain Britanov's orders and leadership, the crew of the K-219 was able to successfully bring the crippled submarine to the surface, but the damage was irreparable.

To compound matters further, both of the submarine's OK-700 nuclear reactors began to overheat, forcing Lieutenant N.N. Belikov and a nineteen-year-old engineering technician, Seaman S.A. Preminin, to enter the ship's reactor compartment to manually shutdown the reactors.

After Belikov succumbed to the heat inside the reactor compartment, Preminin continued working alone and succeeding in manually lowering the control rods, shutting down both reactors. However, he unfortunately became trapped inside the compartment and suffocated. His actions prevented a nuclear catastrophe which would have impacted the entire Eastern seaboard of the United States.

The exercise of the simple basic freedom of speech could have prevented the K-219 disaster and subsequent loss of life, but it had been ripped away by the power-blinded eyes of communist mentality instilling silence from the crew due to the fear of reprisal from the authoritarian leadership of the state.

In Canada, recent laws enacting extreme speech codes allow freedom of speech for liberal voices but make the expression of conservative views all but illegal. In China, those who speak out against government policies run the risk of imprisonment or worse. Why is the suppression of freedom of speech such a powerful force in the realm of Socialism? The reason is simple: Socialism cannot survive without intimidation, propaganda, and the protection of forces loyal to the state.

Socialism eventually leads to the establishment of a government which is increasingly tyrannical in nature. Just like oil and water do not mix, freedom and socialism do not mix. The more socialist a nation becomes, the fewer freedoms its citizens will enjoy. A nation of people who possess the freedom to criticize the failure of their government will be viewed as an enemy of that government and will be treated as such. In order to counteract a negative view of its policies and practices, a socialist government requires an extensive bureaucracy which will grow from a tiny, annoying insect into a frightening monster which becomes harder and harder to kill.

Another negative impact of Socialism lies in its divisive nature. Socialism thrives on turning a nation's people against one another. If a nation's citizens are engaged in conflicts between disagreeing viewpoints, they will not be so focused on disagreeing with and speaking out against the government. No one in their right mind who has been successful and has reaped the rewards of their labor would willing agree to allow the state to take away their possessions and give them to someone else. Therefore, one of Socialism's ploys is to create a class of victims who can be indoctrinated to view the successful as their evil enemies.

Under the ebbing tide of Socialist influence, the United States is becoming a nation which is increasingly divided. Various issues have been exploited by socialist legislatures for the sole purpose of dividing the nation's people, thereby making it easier for them to slowly and carefully increase their presence within American society and government. From everything from abortion to gun control, Socialists have endeavored to drive the wedge of division deeper and deeper into American society, and their efforts will continue as long as the American people allow them to continue until the nation will eventually wake up one morning to realize the government which was intended to be "of the people, by the people, and for the people" will have become the exact opposite: a government of the government, by the government, and for the government.

In a speech delivered in Springfield, Illinois on June 16, 1858, Abraham Lincoln, who would later become president of the United States, quoting from the Holy Bible, made the famous statement: "*A house divided against itself cannot stand.*" The pursued division of a society instigated by a Socialist government will become the terminal disease which leads to a nation's demise.

Finally, Socialism tends to create an imbalance of justice and consideration within a society in that Socialism believes the end justifies the means; regardless of whether the efforts used to achieve the end are right or wrong. Socialism's ultimate goal of protecting itself, and rules, regulations, laws, and process tends to be interpreted differently by Socialism's proponents. Socialists proponents typically believe in one set of rules and laws for their subjects and a different set of rules for themselves. For example, former Cuban dictator Fidel Castro led a communist revolution against the evil and corrupt rich citizens of Cuba seemingly to advance the case of the poor; however, he was later learned to be worth approximately nine hundred million dollars. Such hypocrisy is rampant in Socialist bureaucracies.

Socialism is only positive to its proponents who are successful in gaining power, lounging under the protective umbrella of a centralized government, and protected by a force of purchased loyal defenders. For the rest of the population, Socialism is an oppressive, divisive, and enslaving force which delivers nothing of what its supporters promise. Socialism typically abandons the rule of law, at least in respect to itself, because the rule of law tends to hinder Socialism's ambitions. Under such corruption, a nation degenerates into a culture plagued with violence, protests, and recurring revolutions as its people struggle to throw off the yoke of oppression which binds them in hopeless despair.

CHAPTER SIX

THE END RESULT OF SOCIALISM

Socialism tends to eventually reveal itself as a dry well of empty promises, and a wolf in sheep's clothing, as it lunges forth from the underbrush of disguise to overpower and subdue its unsuspecting prey. Nation after nation has allowed socialism to gain a foothold slowly but surely on its society, only to find itself in the path of disaster like a mountain village in the path of an avalanche. Countless individuals have risked their very lives to escape from the chains of a socialist bureaucracy, and many have paid with their lives for the attempt. If Socialism is so wonderful, why do so many seek to escape the clutches of its grasp?

In the 1980s, a young woman from El Salvador came to the United States in search of a new life. She confided to an American journalist that socialism and related systems pretend to care for the poor but rather tend to enslave entire nations. She explained the proponents of socialism first work their way into a society by indoctrination and offering of a system which is supposed to care for the poor and provide equality. But after the people are deceived into believing the socialist propaganda and are persuaded to accept it, those who forced socialism onto a society then transform the system to suit their own needs, desires, and agendas.

In an interview with Brenda Huffmann (AXcess News), this El Salvadorian woman described her experience in El Salvador and her efforts to escape the carnage of Socialist influence. During the interview, this young El Salvadorian woman (name withheld for personal protection) described the devastating chain of events which transpired as Socialism gained an ever-increasing hold over her former country. She stated that, under the influence and instigation of socialism, a small business where her mother worked as an accountant was driven to shut down, her father—a university chemist—found his salary reduced to a fraction of what it was, and his paychecks became more sporadic instead of more consistent; businesses were driven out of the country, and job creation stagnated; taxes were drastically increased, and land and individual wealth was redistributed against the will of those who had worked for and earned the fruits of their labor.

During the interview, she went on to say the conditions deteriorated far beyond the events already described. Socialist proponents and sympathizers encouraged people to kill business owners in an effort to punish the wealthy for their war of inequality against the poor; the health care system was socialized as a promise for health care for all people, but instead, countless people died while they were placed on waiting list for government approval to consult a physician or receive certain medical tests. Hunger due to food shortages became an epidemic and people were stripped of their freedom of choice, even to the point of being instructed and directed as to how they were to educate their children.

In addition, the freedom of worship was all but eliminated. The young El Salvadorian immigrant's testimony painted a very grim picture of the reality of socialism's impact on a society, a nation, and individual citizens. She went on to describe how the message of socialism was pushed into the minds of younger El Salvadorians through schools and universities in the name of social justice and equality. The efforts and manipulations of socialist proponents in El Salvador created a system of class warfare and national disunity.

By the 1970s, socialist proponents who had worked to brainwash the masses into accepting their false message of socialist hope began more violent campaigns aimed at public transportation resources, radio stations were highjacked and used to spread socialist propaganda over the airwaves, and national and foreign businessmen and women were kidnapped and assassinated.

After realizing her only solution was to escape from a crumbling nation, this young woman from El Salvador was forced to leave her young son behind while she came to the United States. After a period of time, she was able to bring her son to America, complete her GED and eventually earned a bachelor's degree. At the time of her interview, she had been married for twelve years and added two stepchildren to her family. But El Salvador is not the only example of the failure of Socialism on a national level.

In 1997, Zimbabwe was hailed as one of the most productive and wealthiest nations on the continent of Africa. Today, the nation is in the throes of utter chaos and disaster, largely due to the policies and actions of its former president, Robert Mugabe.

Mugabe was born in Zimbabwe's predecessor nation—Rhodesia, in 1924. At the time, Southern Rhodesia was a British colony. After his father mysteriously disappeared when Mubabe was still a child, he assisted his mother is caring for their family. Thanks to Jesuit missionaries, Mugabe received a higher level of education than many of his peers. Mugabe later studied in South Africa and eventually earned a BA degree in history and English in 1951. He then returned to Rhodesia where he worked as a teacher. In 1953, Mugabe completed a bachelor's of education degree by correspondence courses. He would later go on to earn a BS degree in economics through correspondence courses with the University of London.

While living and working in the nation of Ghana, Mugabe stated in 1961 he had embraced the ideologies of Marxism. He returned to Rhodesia where he endeavored to convert his home country to Marxism and its beliefs. One of his initial goals was to drive out the white British colonials who in his mind had enslaved the nation.

In 1961, Mugabe and his supporters founded the Zimbabwe African People's Union (ZAPU) in the neighboring nation of Tanzania. The organization soon grew to a total membership of more than 450,000. Mugabe was later arrested in Southern Rhodesia and was detained in various detention facilities before eventually being incarcerated in Salisbury Prison. When change did not come immediately through political efforts, Mugabe utilized covert communications to incite a guerrilla war with the intention of liberating Southern Rhodesia from British Rule.

Mugabe was released from prison in 1974 with the permission of then Prime Minister Ian Smith who was loyal to the British Colonial government. Smith had granted Mugabe permission to attend a conference in Lusaka, Zambia (former Northern Rhodesia). Mugabe used his leave from prison to affect an escape to Southern Rhodesia and reform his guerrilla army. Through the remainder of the 1970s, a bloody civil war raged throughout the region.

By 1979, with Zimbabwe's economy in a shamble, Prime Minister Smith attempted to reach an agreement with Mugabe and his supporters to move forward with the transfer of Zimbabwe's government to a black majority rule. Zimbabwe gained total independence from British rule in 1980 and became an independent state. That same year, Mugabe ran successfully for the office of prime minister under the ZANU (Zimbabwe African National Union) party, but he still faced an uphill battle. The ZANU and ZAPU parties in Zimbabwe had differing agendas, and in 1981 a new outbreak of fighting erupted. The murder of several missionaries by some of Mugabe's forces in 1987 finally brought the opposing sides to the realization of the need to end the fighting. In a loose and somewhat uneasy alliance, the ZANU and ZAPU parties were merged into the ZANU-Patriotic Front (ZANU-PF). Within a week of the signing of the Zimbabwe Unity Agreement, Mugabe was appointed as prime minister of the new government in Zimbabwe, and he selected Joshua Nkomo, his former opponent, as a senior minister.

Embracing an agenda to revive the nation's economy, drive out white Zimbabweans, and push the country from a capitalist to a socialist style of government, Mugabe went to work. From 1994 to 1996, Mugabe's policies brought some initial relief to the nation's struggling economy, specifically through manufacturing, mining, and farming related businesses. Schools and clinics for Zimbabwe's black population were also established. However, some of Mugabe's actions, including the confiscation of the land of white owners while providing no compensation, began to cause dissatisfaction among Zimbabwe's population. In addition, Mugabe refused to amend the single-party constitution of Zimbabwe, economic inflation was increasing, and Zimbabwe's political leaders granted themselves self-appointed pay raises. As the 1990s passed, the Zimbabwe public displayed increasing resentment toward Mugabe and his government as food production, due to improperly trained farmers who had been provided with land seized from experience European farmers, dropped to almost half of what was needed to supply the country's population. Inflation soared to 80,000,000,000 percent, and according to the World Bank, Zimbabwe's GDP dropped by over two billion dollars. In addition, Mugabe's military activities in the Congo did nothing to help the nation's economic dilemma.

Zimbabwe's foreign relations also began to deteriorate in 2000, when Mugabe pushed through an amendment to Zimbabwe's constitution, ordering Great Britain to pay financial reparations because of land seized from black Rhodesians during the colonial period and threatened to seize British property in reprisal if the British government failed to comply with his demands. Mugabe had also attempted to persuade foreign nations to donate money to assist with land distribution but met without success when he refused to accept the terms of agreement proposed by various nations in return for their monetary support.

Many European government officials suspected Mugabe had stuffed the ballot box in order to win the 2002 Zimbabwe presidential election. Numerous sanctions were placed on Zimbabwe including an arms embargo. By this time, the nation's economy was wrecked, and a severe famine, an AIDs epidemic, high unemployment, and a huge foreign debt compounded an already catastrophic problem. Nevertheless, Mugabe was determined to retain his office regardless of what it might require.

In 2005, Mugabe was again re-elected president of Zimbabwe, although many people alleged he did so through corrupt practices and violence directed toward any opponents and dissidents. Throughout his term, Zimbabwe's condition failed to improve, and Mugabe faced increasing competition from a new political party: The Movement for Democratic Change (MDC) led by Morgan Tsvangirai. Finally, after twenty-eight years of violence, economic chaos, corruption, and empty promises of hope, the people of Zimbabwe had had enough.

On March 28, 2008 Mugabe was defeated by Tsvangirai in his bid to retain his position as president of Zimbabwe, but Mugabe refused to accept the outcome of the election and insisted on a recount of the votes. During the month of May of that year, Mugabe's followers violently attacked and murdered a large number of the MDC, and Mugabe publicly stated he would not relinquish control of the country to Tsvangirai. A run-off election was held in June of 2008, but the bitter resistance of Mugabe and the risk of further dividing the nation through violent efforts to force his resignation, Tsvangirai elected to withdraw from the race.

Mugabe's stubborn resistance to relinquish power ignited a new wave of violence which swept the nation of Zimbabwe resulting in thousands of casualties. Despite a temporary power-sharing agreement between Mugabe and Tsvangirai to curb the violence and unrest, Mugabe managed to maintain a strong hold over the government. His efforts continued through 2010. Another election was held in 2013 but was again disrupted by corrupt activities on violence on Mugabe's part.

In August of 2013, the election commission of Zimbabwe officially declared Mugabe the winner, although the opposition accused election officials who were quite likely controlled by Mugabe's supporters of discarding over seventy thousand ballots. In November of 2017, the Zimbabwe military began mobilization efforts with the intent of removing Mugabe from power. The Parliament of Zimbabwe met on November 22nd of that year with Mugabe's impeachment at the top of their agenda, and the embittered president finally conceded defeat, although he would continue to voice arguments and incite unrest within the nation. Today, Zimbabwe is an impoverished and struggling nation scared by past violence and plagued with a decimated economy, all caused by the ambitions of a socialist totalitarian ruler.

A more recent example of the failure and oppressive reality of Socialism may be observed by the catastrophe currently occurring in the South American nation of Venezuela. Once a country with a strong economy, thanks in part to its valuable petroleum resources, Venezuela was launched down the downward spiraling road of socialism by a man named Hugo Chavez and is now a nation teetering on the brink of economic, social, and humanitarian disaster.

Hugo Chavez was born on July 28, 1954 in Sabaneta, Venezuela. Chavez later obtained a degree from the Venezuelan Academy of Military Sciences in 1975 and became a paratrooper in the Venezuelan military.

Over time, Chavez and many of his military associates grew dissatisfied with the efforts of then President Carlos Andres Perez. Perez's period of leadership was repeatedly marred by accusation of corruption and misuse of funds. Interestingly, Perez served three consecutive terms as vice president in an organization known as the Socialist International, which contributed to the promotion of socialism throughout Latin America. Continued dissention eventually led to an attempted coup in February of 1992, which was led by then Lieutenant-Colonel Hugo Chavez. Though unsuccessful, the cease-fire called for by Chavez proved to be only temporary, and in November of that same year, a second coup attempt was launched which also failed. Chavez served a short prison sentence before being granted a pardon.

In March of the following year, Perez was accused of embezzlement by Venezuelan Attorney General Ramon Escovar Salom. The accusation was eventually deemed to be valid, and after several weeks of resisting a call to resign, Perez was removed from office by the Venezuelan National Congress in August of 1993. He later died of respiratory failure in 2010.

Venezuela's journey down the road toward socialism probably began prior to Hugo Chavez, but he was certainly a catalyst to the reaction. After a successful campaign for office in 1998, Chavez took office as president of Venezuela in 1999. He promised to combat corruption within the Venezuelan government and bring about reforms with the goal of boosting the sagging Venezuelan economy. During his first year in office, Chavez embarked on a successful mission to amend congressional and judicial powers granted by the nation's constitution.

As time went by, Chavez strengthened his personal authority over Venezuela's state-run petroleum company, resulting in numerous protest and objections by certain military officials. Chavez became an increasingly outspoken critic of the United States and threatened to stop supplying America with petroleum. Chavez also supported socialist guerrilla forces operating in neighboring Latin American countries and adamantly opposed operations against South American drug cartels. As Chavez continued to push his campaign of moving Venezuela away from a capitalist form of government, he stated that he was convinced that the path to a new, better and possible world did not lie with capitalism but rather with socialism.

Opposition to some of Chavez's policies resulted in the emergence of numerous enemies among the people of Venezuela. On more than one occasion, efforts were made to remove him from office. Due to growing unrest and opposition to his efforts by certain factions within the Venezuelan population, Chavez endeavored to take action which would reduce the threat against him.

In 2012, Chavez pushed the Venezuelan National Assembly to pass a piece of legislation which became known as the Control of Arms, Munitions and Disarmament Law, with the intention of disarming all the citizens of Venezuela. When the law went into effect in 2013, the commercial sale of firearms and ammunition was made illegal except for certain government officials. Initially, Chavez tried a voluntary turn-in program in which citizens could trade their weapons for various electrical appliances; however, the government recorded only thirty-seven cases of voluntary firearm surrender.

When his amnesty program failed, Chavez resorted to another more aggressive effort to disarm the people of Venezuela, and over time, nearly thirteen thousand weapons were seized from Venezuelan citizens by force. Chavez added salt to open wounds by publicly displaying the destruction of those firearms on Venezuelan television.

Initially, most of the Venezuelan people fell for the message of security and equality preached by Chavez from his socialist pulpit. It did not take long for them to realize their hopes had been in vain.

The Venezuelan government established gangs throughout the nation to instill fear in the people. Police forces did little to protect the population from criminal activities, and the crime rate in Venezuela soared. The number of homicides in Venezuela rose from 6,500 in 2001 to nearly 28,000 in 2015, making the nation's murder rate the highest around the world.

In 2011, Hugo Chavez was diagnosed with cancer, and despite multiple operations, his condition continued to deteriorate. Realizing he would be unable to continue serving in office due to his failing health, Chavez appointed his vice president, Nicolas Maduro, to take over the duties of president of Venezuela. Chavez finally succumbed to his illness and died in 2013. Maduro would pick up the reins of socialism wielded by Chavez and continue driving the nation down the road to self-destruction.

Maduro continued to utilize pro-government forces to locate and seize personal firearms and punish those who possessed them. Since Maduro came to power in 2014, Venezuela has increased the rate of its downward economic spiral and internal social unrest and dissention. The nation's economy has literally self-destructed and is no longer able to sustain itself or provide for the population.

While large numbers of Venezuela's population have elected to flee the country, others have attempted to stand up against government oppression but with tragic results. In 2017, on several occasions, pro-democracy protesters campaigned to do away with the crumbling socialist regime in Venezuela. Their efforts were thwarted by government security forces, and over time, some two hundred Venezuelans have been killed attempting to bring change to their dying nation. Attacking soldiers with guns while armed only with rocks is not normally an effective strategy. David Kopel, an adjunct professor and political analyst, suggested that the Venezuelan dictatorship views the possession of firearms as a risk and danger to the establishment of a total monopoly of power typical of socialist and/or communist governments. Today, with hundreds of its citizens being shot and killed in the streets by their own military and millions of others seeking refuge in neighboring nations, Venezuela's national condition has deteriorated to a condition of total chaos. Limited food supplies, medical supplies and treatment accessibility, high unemployment, and runaway inflation are killing a nation that was once one of the wealthiest in South America.

Everywhere the vessel of socialism has sailed, catastrophe has followed in its wake. Now, the stage is being set for the same tragedy to be repeated in the United States of America. The increasing number of socialist proponents in American government offices and positions has created a growing risk for the Land of the Free and the Home of the Brave to become a socialist wasteland.

With America's educational institutions becoming increasingly staffed by pro-socialist administrators and educators, America's young adults who attend these institutions of higher learning are being increasingly indoctrinated instead of educated, resulting in the appearance of a cancer of naivety and complacency within the generation which will one day lead this nation: a generation which has no concept of the dark days of the Cold War and the Iron Curtain; the lack of freedom to speak one's mind freely without fear of repercussion; the right to oppose corruption and injustice at the government level; and the freedom to worship and practice one's faith in peace.

America's younger generation is being deceived into embracing socialism in ever increasing numbers without any conception, understanding, or fear of what such a government will bring. Unless the American people open their eyes to the truth, the nation is racing at ever-increasing speed down a dead-end road which will only lead to self-destruction.

Chapter Seven

The Emergence of Socialism in the United States

The United States of America, regardless of any crisis, tragedy, or situation it had been subjected to, is a blessed nation. Over the course of its 240 some odd years of existence, America has been spared from the violence, chaos, oppression, and subjugation which has been inflicted on the people of other less fortunate nations around the world. Our distance from potentially hostile aggressors and the expanse of two vast oceans has served to protect us from many of our enemies, or at least have made it much more difficult for an enemy to reach us, and with the exception of the British forces during the War of 1812, no enemy military force has ever gained a strong foothold on sovereign United States territory.

However, over the past several decades, the geographical and political barriers which have shielded our nation in the past have been breached, and the enemy is already within our borders and is digging its claws into every avenue of American society. This "silent invasion" has successfully occurred without the American people ever realizing what was happening.

In approximately 539 BC, the Persian army stood before the massively fortified city of Babylon with its thick, massive, and seemingly unbreachable walls. The Babylonian king, Belshazzar, celebrated his supposed security with a massive feast augmented by copious amounts of wine until, according to the

Bible, a hand appeared and wrote a message on the palace wall which none of Belshazzar's servants could interpret. Finally, the Prophet Daniel read the message and informed Belshazzar that very night Babylon would be conquered, and he would be killed. The message was certainly difficult to believe, but the Persian army executed an incredible tactical feat: they diverted the Euphrates River which flowed through the heart of the city, marched underneath the city wall, and defeated one of the most powerful nations on earth in a single night.

Ironically, over 2,500 years later, this episode of history has repeated itself in the United Stated of America. The serpent of socialism has slithered silently, stealthfully, and secretively into American society and is gaining an ever-increasing influence over an increasingly unwary population, and those who embrace the concept of socialism often have no idea what they are supporting. Infatuated by the words and messages of socialism's proponents, many of America's younger population have fallen for the repetitive lie of socialism's promise of equality, prosperity, and security for all the nation's citizens. They have no idea that what they will receive is the exact opposite.

In the latter part of the nineteenth century, the ideology of socialism began to spread its roots into American soil. German immigrants, some with socialist beliefs, began to arrive in the United States in the late 1850s. These individuals eventually formed Marxian socialist unions. Some of these included the National Typographic Union, formed in 1852; United Hatters, which was formed in 1856, as well as others.

In 1900, the Socialist Party became an open and public entity in the United States, and in just over a decade, numerous professed socialists had managed to win election to public office. These included the office of mayor in Milwaukee, Wisconsin; Berkley, California; and Schenectady, New York, in addition of at least one congressman, 145 aldermen, and around 160 city council members. Before long, the Socialist Party in America numbered in excess of one hundred thousand.

One of American socialism's earliest key leaders was a man named Eugene V. Debs from Indiana, who led the party during 1912. Socialists also published several newspapers, including the Kansas-based paper *Appeal of Reason* which boasted over a half-a-million subscribers. Debs was a very dynamic leader and appealed to many of his peers. In the 1912 presidential election, Debs ran against Theodore Roosevelt and William Howard Taft. Debs lost his bid to become president of the United States, but he did receive approximately nine hundred thousand votes. During the first twenty years of the twentieth century, the number of socialists running for public office gradually increased. In addition, socialists began to reach out and lure in the young people of the United States in an effort to plant the seed of their ideology into the minds of those who would later find themselves in positions to promote and enact the socialist agenda.

The indoctrination of socialism into the minds of young adults by America's institution of higher learning is not a recent issue. American writer Upton Sinclair played a major role in establishing the Intercollegiate Socialist Society and planting chapters in many of the nation's major colleges and universities. By 1905, the Intercollegiate Socialist Society was well implanted in the university culture and unwary students were being introduced to the New Gospel according to Saint Marx. Remember, Marx envisioned a society in which God or faith had no place. Universities today continue the effort to suppress student expression of practice of faith and criticize young people's commitment to religious beliefs, especially Christian beliefs.

Despite setbacks which occurred during the years spanning the First World War, socialism in America refused to disappear. Eugene Debs ran for the office of President of the United States again in 1920 and received over 919,000 votes.

Debs' efforts in promoting socialism eventually led to his being viewed as a possible threat to national security. He was eventually arrested but later pardoned in 1921 by President Warren G. Harding. Debs died before he could run for office again, but in 1928, another socialist, Norman Thomas, ran for president. However, Thomas only received approximately 260,000 votes. Divisions over various issues continued to plague the Socialist Party in America but failed to destroy it. Despite the embrace of socialism by some elements of American society, not everyone fell for the deceptive message of the left.

Writer F. A. Hayek published a book in 1944 entitled *The Road to Serfdom* in which he addressed a concern to which some people had given the name: Creeping Socialism. In his book, Hayek expressed concerns and delivered dire warnings over many of the dangers which he saw lurking just over America's horizon, which included the idea of various means of production being placed under state control.

During the decade of the 1950s, support for communism and socialism took a drastic plunge due to the horrors of World War Two, the Cold War against communism which followed, and other issues. In addition, the birth of the atomic bomb gave rise to a whole new fear of socialism and communism influence and expansion, especially after Russia exploded its first nuclear weapon in 1949. Also, improved working conditions, salaries, and lifestyles caused many Americans who once pondered the so-called positive aspects of socialism to change alliances to the Democratic Party. Many former would-be socialists began to feel that progressive reform could be better achieved through the efforts of the Democratic Party than through the increasingly distrusted Socialist Party.

For a period of approximately twenty years, the socialist movement in the United States all but disappeared. Internal conflicts within the Socialist Party in America over exactly what to support and whose leadership should be followed greatly hindered the Socialist Party's ability to function. Also, there existed a diverse pattern of ideologies within the Socialist Party as a whole. Certain groups professing socialism leaned toward extremist views of Neo-Nazism and a hatred of the state of Israel. Some of these groups which huddled under the umbrella of what was referred to as the National Socialist Movement (NSM) condoned both violent as well as non-violent approaches to promoting and obtaining their agenda. While extremist views are and should be a serious concern, such ideologies and their related actions are easy to identify and counter. Any group which promotes and carries out violent acts in support of their mission will inevitably step outside the bounds of the law and eventually find themselves in serious legal trouble.

While the efforts of extremist socialism is obvious, another group which claims socialist support is showing itself to be far more dangerous due to its somewhat benevolent approach to gaining influence and support among the American population, especially through the many intellectually brainwashed graduates emerging in ever greater numbers from America's institutions of higher learning. Many younger people today are rejecting the values, morals, and self-discipline of their fathers and mothers while embracing the deceptive teachings of many socialist/secularist university professors. Faith, family, and patriotism are taking a back seat to self-centered desires and ambitions. The disrespect for parental authority, civil authority, legal authority, and American flag by many young people and young adults in America today is crippling American society and planting the seeds for a complete degeneration of American culture. A group which is exploiting the deteriorating value system of younger Americans is the Socialist Party U.S.A.

The Socialist Party U.S.A. is a group which sometimes refers to their ideology as "Democratic Socialism." Their message is a desire and so-called promise to create a political and economic system which allows equality and freedom for all citizens, enabling Americans to develop and fulfill their full potential while at the same time existing in harmony with the rest of society. The Democratic Socialists assure people through their passive but deceptive actions they believe in and are committed to the basic freedoms guaranteed by the United States Constitution: Freedom of Speech, Freedom of Assembly, Freedom of the Press, Freedom of Religion, and the continuation of a multi-party political system which allows all views and concerns to be expressed, acknowledged, and protected.

However, their message, like any other offer of socialism, comes with an olive leaf in the visible hand and a concealed weapon of oppression in the other. Over the years, facts and circumstances have repeatedly shown that socialism cannot exist without some oppressive guard to protect it. Sooner or later, at least some people will grow wise as to what socialism actually stands for and openly resist it. Regardless of what kind of message of peace, equality, and respect socialists preach, their desire is absolute control on their terms, and they will do whatever it takes to obtain that power.

Anyone who as ever contracted a common cold knows the process of going from feeling fine to being in misery. First, there is the slow but increasing lack of energy, followed by the sudden sinus issues, headaches, and other symptoms. Within a short time, the full effects of the common cold hit with a vengeance, hangs on like a leech, and relentlessly resists being driven away.

This is exactly how socialism is working its way deeper and deeper into the roots of American society. At first, everything seems okay, then a few concerns arise. Eventually, the painful reality strikes. Many people who are complacent about political issues do not even realize the reality of socialism's growing presence in the United States, nor do they understand the eventual results of a socialist-controlled America.

There is an old saying: Complacency Kills! There is no question the complacency towards the growing emergence of socialism in America will result in a surprised shock to millions of people who lay down at night to sleep in the land of the free and the home of the brave, then wake up to a new dawn revealing America to be a land of the suppressed and the home of the oppressed. Throughout history, the fall of many nations and empires has occurred while populations of those nations turned a deaf ear and a blind eye to the actions of the present and a nonchalant attitude towards the dark possibilities of tomorrow.

A tragic reality lies in the fact that in twenty-first century America, just as the Babylonians discovered in the dark of the night in 539 BC, the enemy is already within the walls. Socialism is alive, present, and a growing in influence in the United States, and its proponents, with the assistance of many of America's institutions of higher learning, are gaining a growing number of unwary supporters, most of whom do not realize what they are really supporting and likely will not gain that realization until it is too late. One sign of the increasing grip of socialism on America may be viewed in the actions and attitudes of the younger generation.

As mentioned earlier in this book, America has not, is not, and will never be a perfect nation. From our Founding Fathers to our present-day leaders, America has made its share of mistakes, bad decisions, and is guilty of actions condemned by the very foundational values America was founded on. But nevertheless, America is a great nation, and it has proven itself a faithful friend to many oppressed people around the world. But many people emerging into adulthood in America have been indoctrinated with the concept that a utopian society can be created in our country, such as those envisioned by the earliest proponents of socialism.

Also, regardless of what modern-day secular humanist leaders and promoters in America say or believe, the values of a nation compose its foundation. The Pilgrims came to America searching for a place where they could worship God and profess and promote their faith without the influences and hindering resistance of the Church of England. Socialists strongly support the freedom of religion, but recent actions have clearly shown they do not support the freedom of Christianity. Socialists also strongly support the freedom of speech, except for those professing Christianity or anti-socialist sentiments. In addition, socialists promote the freedom of choice except for those choosing to practice and promote Christian beliefs or reject socialist ideology. Socialists support freedom of assembly but primarily for the support of their own mission.

Repeatedly across the years of recent American history, those who offer any opposition to and disagreement with socialist ideology are harassed, threatened, persecuted, belittled, and even punished by the very courts which are required by law to protect their rights.

In the former Soviet Union, dissidents who spoke out against communism were persecuted, imprisoned, and even killed. The Party was the only god to whom anyone could bow before in reverence. The will of the Party, or rather the will of those who compose the Party leadership, was the law of the land, a law interpreted by personal opinions instead of checked against a governing document such as the Constitution. The withholding of the truth from the population was a power tool in suppressing unrest and dissention. The less people knew about reality, the less likely they were to question it. And when people did question communism's reality and its efforts, they were quickly and harshly dealt with as deterrent to others who might consider the same course of action.

This same plan of suppression and totalitarianism is being developed today in the United States of America. America is a nation which has remained free for almost two and a half centuries, and America has remained free thus far due to a variety of factors. Those factors are under increasing attack by the proponents of socialism because they know their system will never survive in the face of any type of opposition.

As the influence of socialism creeps ever deeper into American society, its cancerous effects are becoming more and more obvious and in ever increasing clarity; the writing on the wall is becoming visible.

CHAPTER EIGHT

THE CURRENT CRISIS

An increasingly secular mindset is fertilizing the soil of American society in preparation for the sowing of a crop of socialism which may prove extremely difficult to defend against in the years to come. There exists an increasing possibility that, a few generations from now, the United States which was founded with a government of the people, by the people, and for the people with the rights of the people protected by a democratically created and approved Constitution may no longer exist as we know it today. America would not be the first culture to be swallowed up and digested by an internal invasive power bent on total domination of a nation and a people.

America was once a nation of values, but the commitment to those values is dissolving away in the current and coming generations of American citizens. One of the most important values which is fading away is the value of human life: specifically, the lives of the unborn.

On August 26, 1910 a baby girl named Anjezë Gonxhe Bojaxhiu was born in Skopje, a city of the Ottoman Empire in a region later to become known as Albania. She chose to become a nun when she was eighteen years old and devoted the remainder of her life to missionary work in the form of helping and ministering to others who were in need and all but forgotten about by others. She would later become known as Mother Teresa.

Standing barely five feet tall, Mother Teresa was no giant in stature, but her message to the world through her actions and words was truly mountainous.

Never one to mince words, Mother Teresa once made a truly profound and certainly controversial statement: *"Any country that accepts abortion is the poorest of the poor."* (Mother Teresa, 1994)

Abortion has always been and always will be a difficult and controversial subject. While certain medical conditions or situations may certainly merit the need for abortion, a vast majority of abortions are performed for two reasons: (1) monetary gain, and (2) a desire to dispose of an unwanted and/or unplanned responsibility. Abortion was declared legal by the United States Supreme Court in 1973, composed of Chief Justice Warren E. Burger, and Associate Justices William O. Douglas, William J. Brennan Jr., Potter Stewart, Byron White, Thurgood Marshall, Harry Blackmun, Lewis F. Powell Jr., and William Rehnquist. In the 7-2 vote which made Roe vs. Wade law, Chief Justice Burger, and associate justices Douglas, Brennan, Stewart, Marshall, Blackman, and Powell voted in favor of the case, while associate justices White and Rehnquist dissented.

In the aftermath of this critical Supreme Court decision, between 1973 to 2010, more than fifty-three million abortions have been performed legally in the United States alone. That total exceeds the number of combat related deaths suffered by the United States Military in the American Revolutionary War, the War of 1812, the Mexican-American War (1846-1848), the American Civil War, World War I, World War II, the Korean War, the War in Vietnam, the Iraq War, and the War in Afghanistan combined. It is no wonder some people have suggested the most dangerous place for a child in America to be is inside its mother's womb. In the shadow of Mother Teresa's wisdom, even with a Gross National Product of over nineteen trillion dollars (2017), the United States of America is surely the poorest nation in the world.

Modern day Democratic Socialists and closet socialists have rallied around the concept of what they refer to as "Freedom of Choice." In other words, the freedom of an individual to elect to end the life of an unborn child for any reason, medically necessary or not. They preach health and prosperity without ever referring to the traumatic events which occur during an abortion.

Just as socialism destroys an individual's desire to succeed and better themselves because they have a right to do whatever they want and someone else has an obligation to support them, socialism also destroys the value of human life.

When I was a child, I remember my grandparents having an RCA console black and white television set. This antiquated piece of technology used electronic vacuum tubes which occasionally failed. On many occasions, I remember riding to the local store with my grandfather and watched him insert a failed tube into a device known as a tube tester, verify the tube was bad, and purchase a new one for replacement. With simple repairs such as this, that old RCA television lasted for over eighteen years!

Today, we live in a disposable society. Disposable plates, cups, razors, tools, diapers, eyeglasses…even disposable people! A society which is indoctrinated to believe in the morality of throwing away unborn children like they were yesterday's garbage is certainly headed down a road to disaster.

Modern day socialists who are rising to prominence in American governmental positions at every level have no real regard for human life or constitutional law. Like any socialist or communist proponent, they are only concerned with forcing their agenda on the population for their own personal interest and gain. The problem for them is that not everyone in the United States is in favor of socialism, and that fact stands as an unpleasant and unwanted obstacle to the socialist onslaught in America. In response to this obstacle, socialist proponents in the United States have in recent years attempted to capitalize on tragedies to force the removal of a major factor composing that obstacle. Their efforts are centered around a massive movement involving an attack against the very Constitution which they and all elected leaders swear a solemn oath to support and defend. That movement is commonly referred to as Gun Control.

The Second Amendment to the United States Constitution, a requirement for many of the original states to vote for its ratification, is not amendable or revocable. The Constitution and the Bill of Rights are the foundation of American government, ratified and approved by the original thirteen colonies. Without the first ten amendments to the Constitution, this governing document which has stood longer than any other of its kind in history, would have never been ratified.

During the Second World War, the United States faced a sudden and terrifying reality. In the early morning hours of December 7, 1941, the United States Pacific Fleet was all but crippled at the outset of hostilities by a well planned and executed surprise attack mounted by the naval and aviation forces of the Empire of Japan. However, even with their unexpected advantage initially gained by their victory at Pearl Harbor, the Japanese leadership never chose to attempt an invasion of the United States mainland. Their reason was their knowledge of the fact that the majority of the average US citizens were armed, and even if Japanese forces were successful in gaining a foothold on the West Coast, they knew they would never succeed in making any progress Eastward, for in their path would stand farmers, store owners, businessmen, law enforcement officials, housewives, mechanics, and a host of everyday people who have been blessed by their Founding Fathers with the irrevocable right to keep and bear arms.

Since the close of 2005, firearms sales in the United States have increased drastically. According to the US Federal Bureau of Investigation, gun sales reached a record growth in 2006, and in the aftermath of that year, data obtained by the FBI indicated that violent crime rates dropped significantly and continue to do so. In addition, crime data compiled and collated by the FBI indicates law-abiding gun owners are not the problem in what socialists refer to as "gun violence."

But facts mean little to socialist proponents who view the Second Amendment as an obstacle to their goal of a socialist dominated America. Rather than focus on facts, socialists use their pulpit to preach their message of gun control to eliminate gun violence and use as justification for their message the tragic mass shootings which have occurred in the past, the weapons used, and the victims of those shootings.

Socialist proponents have utilized these tragic events for advocating the elimination of firearm ownership by American citizens. However, a fact which they fail to acknowledge is this: law abiding citizens did not commit these atrocities—criminals did! Criminals have no regard for any laws, laws relating to firearms or otherwise. No legislation proposed by socialist advocates or their colleagues is capable of preventing such crimes because criminals will obtain firearms by illegal means. Practically all such proposed legislation impacts only one group of people: law abiding citizens.

While violent acts such as mass shooting are deplorable, tragic, and inexcusable, they are not the work of law-abiding citizens. The reality is that of the number of criminal acts involving mass shootings which have occurred in the United States since the decade of the 1950s, practically all of these events have occurred where citizens are banned or subjected to restrictions from their constitutional right to keep and bear arms. Another fact to consider is that in Europe, three of the worst school shootings in history have occurred where some of the strictest firearm laws in the world exist.

MASS SHOOTINGS IN UNITED STATES 1966 to 2016

1966	University of Texas Tower in Austin, TX	Charles Whitman (Age 25) Former Marine	18 Killed	Killed by police
1984	McDonald's restaurant San Ysidro, CA	James Oliver Huberty (Age 41) Unemployed Security Guard	21 Killed	Killed by police
1986	Edmond Post Office Edmond, OK	Patrick Henry Sherill (Postal Worker)	14 Killed	Suicide
1991	Luby's Cafeteria in Killeen, TX	George Hennard (Age 35)	23 Killed	Suicide
1999	Columbine High School Littleton, CO	Eric Harris & Dylan Klebold (Columbine students)	13 Killed 24 Injured	Suicide
2007	Virginia Tech in Blacksburg, VA	Seung-Hui Cho (Age 23)	32 Killed, 17 Injured	Suicide
2009	American Civic Association, Binghamton, N.Y.	Jiverly Wong, (Age 42) Vietnamese immigrant	13 Killed, 4 Injured	Suicide
2009	Fort Hood Texas	Maj. Nidal Malik Hasan Army psychiatrist	13 Killed, 30 Injured	Apprehended, Sentenced to Death in 2013
2012	Sandy Hook Elementary School Newtown, CT	Adam Lanza	27 Killed (Including his mother prior to attack)	Suicide
2013	Washington Navy Yard in Washington, D.C.	Aaron Alexis (Age 34) Former Navy reservist	12 Killed	Killed by police
2015	Inland Regional Center San Bernardino, CA	Syed Farook (Age 28) & Tashfeen Malik (Age 27)	14 Killed	Both killed in shootout with police
2016	Pulse Orlando nightclub in Orlando, Fla.	Omar Mateen (Age 29)	49 Killed 50+ Injured	Killed in shootout with police

Nations whose leaders have imposed ultra-strict gun control laws have been found through multiple studies to suffer higher murder rates than nations where firearm ownership is supported. One such study revealed that nine European nations with a low percentage of firearm ownership per citizen have seen a combined murder and violent crime rate practically three times higher than nine other European nations with a much higher percentage of citizen who own firearms. One example of firearm ownership reducing crime rates can be found in the efforts made by the citizens and leadership of Kennesaw, Georgia in the United States.

In 1982, in response to a massive number of burglaries having occurred in the city, Kennesaw's leaders passed a law which required the heads of the town's households to maintain at least one firearm in their residence. As a result, the rate of residential burglaries dropped by 89 percent. In the years following, the violent crime rate in Kennesaw, Georgia averaged 85 percent lower than the rest of Georgia's municipalities.

Today, increasing efforts are being made by socialists and their supporters to restrict or eliminate the freedom of citizens not only to own firearms, but to carry them on their persons. Many law-abiding citizens in the United States today carry firearms, either openly or concealed, on their persons. The positive impact of this practice cannot be ignored.

One study conducted by the Federal Bureau of Investigation (FBI) revealed that in states where concealed carry laws had been adopted, murder rates were reduced by approximately 8.5 percent; the number of rapes/sexual assaults was reduced by approximately 5 percent; the number of aggravated assaults was reduced by approximately 7 percent; and the number of robberies was reduced by approximately 3 percent. Other studies have shown that women who have used a gun to defend themselves against sexual abuse or assault approximately two hundred thousand times a year, and three out of five convicted felons who were questioned over the course the FBI study stated they would not consider attempting a crime against an individual who was armed. In an article published by the Foundation for Economic Education, Lawrence W. Reed stated statistics show guns in the hands of law-abiding citizens actually prevent an estimated two and a half million crimes per year!

Despite the efforts made by socialist proponents to paint a gruesome picture of gun ownership and carry as a mass producer of crime and violence, the fact is that, year by year, guns are used approximately eighty thousand times more often to protect or save a life rather than to take a life.

For the past several years, socialists and their colleagues have made an increasing effort over the past several years to exploit such tragedies as mass shootings, especially school shootings, to promote their platform of restricting gun ownership and use by law-abiding citizens in the name of reducing violence; however, their true aim is tied to a critical part of their long-term agenda: the disarming of the American public. Their reason being that an armed American public is a direct obstacle in their path toward totalitarian control over American society. The recent events in the South American nation of Venezuela should be a red flag to all Americans as to what can and will happen if the socialist aim to disarm the American people becomes a reality.

But the threat of socialism to the United States is not limited to internal efforts. In 1945, after the end of World War II, representatives from some fifty nations met in San Francisco, California, and began drafting a charter for a new global organization with an overall goal of conflict resolution through diplomatic means without resulting to warfare. The new organization began operations in October of 1945 and became known as the United Nations. One of the charter nations of the United Nations was the United States which would eventually come to pay approximately 22 percent of the UN budget. Between 1995 and 2005, the United States acquired a debt to the United Nations of $8,881,346,000. And sadly, in its efforts to promote world peace and eliminate warfare, the United Nations has failed miserably.

Since the United Nations began operations, there have been approximately fifty-eight conflicts around the world ranging from full scale wars to regional civil wars and other conflicts; all of which have resulted in the deaths of over forty-five million people. So much for the international effort to eliminate warfare.

A fact that most Americans today are unaware of is that after the end of the Second World War, in 1946, the United States Senate ratified the United Nations Charter as a Treaty Obligation. In the aftermath of this decision, the United States has allowed itself to be hindered, challenged, and, at times, restricted by the United Nations whose leaders over the years have often leaned in favor of supporting the actions of nations who are hostile to America.

Today, the United Nations has become one of the most corrupt organizations on the planet, and the United States provides a vast amount of the funds paid into the UN by its member nations. In addition, another issue which should be of concern to all Americans is that many of the top individuals in authority at the United Nations, including the current UN Secretary General, António Guterres of Portugal, are socialists. Still another issue which should make freedom loving Americans tremble in fear is that the United Nations Charter was drafted by a pair of communist spies who drew much of the United Nations Charter from the "constitution" of the Soviet Union.

While the United Nations stomps back and forth preaching a sermon of world peace and equality for all governments, the UN repeatedly acts with contempt and discrimination toward those who fail to bow in obedience to their will. One example which stands out is the reaction of the United Nations toward the state of Israel following the Entebbe rescue mission.

On June 27, 1976, Palestinian and German terrorists highjacked Air France flight A300, en route from Tel Aviv, Israel, to Paris, France, via Athens, Greece. The terrorists refueled the plane in Libya and then ordered the pilot to fly them to Entebbe, Uganda, where they were reinforced by additional terrorists and the Ugandan Military under the command of President Idi Amin. The terrorists then released the non-Israeli hostages but continued to hold approximately one hundred Israelis along with the French flight crew who refused to leave the remaining hostages behind. Faced with a threat of having one hundred men, women, and children murdered by international criminals, in a bold and daring move, Israel sent a small army 2,500 miles south in C-130 Hercules aircraft, which flew low under hostile radar systems. The force successfully landed at Entebbe, killed all of the terrorists and a large number of Ugandan troops who attempted to interfere with the rescue operation, destroyed eleven Soviet-built Mig 17 and Mig 21 fighter planes to prevent interference from the Ugandan Air Force, and returned home with minimal casualties to the hostages and the members the Israeli Defense Force who took part in the operation.

Rather than praise and congratulate Israel on successfully completing one of the most daring and challenging anti-terrorist operations in history, the United Nations openly condemned Israel for attacking another country. The UN leaders failed to make any firm statement or argument against either the terrorists or Ugandan government which had supported and assisted the terrorists in an international criminal act of war against a sovereign member of the United Nations. Tragically, the voices of criticism raised against Israel for their justified actions included the voice of the United States of America!

Another mostly unknown fact occurred in 1952 when a group of United States Army troops were assigned to the United Nations Command with the task of making practice public firearms confiscations in several American cities.

The road toward disarming the American people continued into the 1960s with an Act passed by the United States Congress and approved by the United States Senate. This act, known as Public Law 87-297, was signed into law by President John F. Kennedy. Under this Public Law 87-297, an organization known as the United States Disarmament Agency was created and empowered to eliminate or transfer all or part of the weapons and/or personnel of the United States armed forces.

In 1959, the University of Michigan established a Center of Research on Conflict Resolution. With the efforts and influence of numerous professors employed by the University of Michigan including Kenneth E. Boulding, Anatole Rapoport, and others who promoted a message and call for total public disarmament, the clandestine efforts toward disarming the American public continued. A few years later in 1962, an International Arms Control Symposium was held in Ann Arbor, Michigan. This symposium was attended by approximately four hundred individuals from government officials to representatives of educational facilities as well as representatives from numerous corporations including Chrysler, Raytheon, General Electric, Lockheed, and representatives from the United States Disarmament Agency. The symposium was also attended by many congressmen, university professors, and even individuals from certain communist front organizations. The symposium was sponsored jointly by the Bendix Corporation and the University of Michigan. Not surprisingly, the Bendix Corporation held a research contract with the United States Disarmament Agency.

The International Arms Control Symposium hosted numerous speakers, the first of which was Victor Karpov. Karpov served as the First secretary of the Soviet Embassy. He was followed by Robert Matteson, a member of the United States Disarmament Agency, and Walther Reuther, then president of the United Auto Workers Union. In all, the symposium hosted ninety-two speakers over the course of four days. Many of these speakers were known communists, supporters of various communist fronts, disarmament proponents, and individuals who were current employees of the United States Disarmament Agency. One of the primary closing endeavors of the International Arms Control Symposium included the persuasion of United States government leaders to put in place laws which, over time, would slowly but surely restrict the private ownership of firearms, a right protected by the Second Amendment, with a long-term goal of complete public firearm confiscation. While such a tragedy has not yet occurred in the United States, the foundation has been laid for this to happen if the American people do not wake up and recognize what has been going on right under the noses of generations spanning almost seven decades.

The idea behind these actions and efforts is that removal of firearms from American Society will eliminate violence and violent crime. This theory has, of course, been repeatedly disproven. Criminals do not abide by the law and hold total disregard for any law prohibiting them from having or using a weapon, whether it be a firearm or something else. Public disarmament will accomplish nothing except to leave the American public at the mercy of criminals.

With the rise of socialism in the ranks of one of the two main American political parties, and the fact that professed socialists are already serving in the Legislative Branch of the United States government, the threat of totalitarian control is growing ever greater. Numerous candidates for the United States 2020 presidential election are open supporters of public disarmament.

Before dropping out of the 2020 presidential race, Robert Francis O'Rourke, who represented the 16th congressional district of Texas, has stated that if he becomes president of the United States, anyone who owns certain types of weapons will be required to sell them to the government. In a tweet sent out in September of 2019, O'Rourke the following statement: "*I was asked how I'd address people's fears that we will take away their assault rifles. I want to be clear; That's exactly what we're going to do.*" (O'Rourke, 2019)

Another guise of socialist aimed at removing access to certain firearms from law abiding citizens is their move from the term "assault weapon" to "military-style weapon." For the most part, socialist proponents have no understanding of the factors which define what an assault weapon is. In the end, socialists do not care what characteristics a firearm has: if it is an obstacle to their agenda—they are opposed to American citizens having access to or possession of any weapons.

The Bureau of Alcohol, Tobacco, Firearms and Explosives (ATF) has published a Firearms Guide—Identification of Firearms Within the Purview of the National Firearms Act. In this document, the ATF clearly spells out the definition of an assault weapon and provides a list of specific types. One critical factor in the definition of an assault weapon is it built with a select fire capability for semi-automatic AND *fully automatic* modes! One of the primary targets of socialists is one of the most popular rifles among American shooting sports enthusiasts today, commonly known as the AR-15.

The AR-15 has been targeted by socialists and their colleagues for the past several years; however, the AR-15 (and variants) by ATF definition is NOT an assault rifle! It does not meet the criteria. Rather, the AR-15 is designated a modern sporting rifle. Granted, the AR-15 looks like a military rifle, but it is not capable of fully automatic select fire, neither can it be mechanically modified for such a function. In addition, the AR-15 has never been issued to the United States military, which uses M-16 and M-4 rifles which can be selected for a fully automatic or three-round burst rate-of-fire. Consider this: A Ford Explorer and a Chevy Tahoe look very much alike, but they are not the same vehicle.

Another misconception of the AR-15 is the idea the letters "AR" stand for "Assault Rifle." Actually, the letters 'AR' stand for ArmaLite Rifle, which was developed by the ArmaLite company during the decade of the 1950s. The AR-15 and other semi-automatic rifles popular with sporting and hunting enthusiasts are not prohibited by the National Firearms Act or the Second Amendment. Most of the socialist-leaning legislators who are so adamantly opposed to American citizens owning modern sporting rifles have a tendency to speak without knowing or acknowledging the facts and have neither the experience, training, qualifications, nor knowledge to know what they are talking about.

Throughout recent history, tragedies have unfortunately been the catalyst for needed change in policy, procedures, and law. After the sinking of the RMS Titanic in 1912, maritime law was changed to require all vessels to carry enough lifeboats for all personnel on board. In 1963, an unforeseen flaw in the design of the emergency main ballast tank blow system on the nuclear-powered attack submarine U.S.S. *Thresher* resulted in the loss of the vessel and all 129 personnel aboard after a flooding casualty in the engine room. The response was the development of the Sub Safe Program, which brought about radical changes in modifications to the design of the flood control equipment utilized with hull openings along with a redesigned emergency main ballast tank blow system. In 1986, the failure of a tiny O-ring in one of the solid rocket boosters of the NASA space shuttle *Challenger* resulted in a post-launch explosion which killed all seven of the astronauts on board. The disaster led to the development of the Quality Assurance Program, which serves to prevent and recognize any mistakes and defects in manufactured parts used in critical systems and tracks those parts from the manufacturer to the workers who install them.

Today, socialists and their cohorts are using the tragedies of mass shootings as an excuse to push for an initial restriction, followed by an eventual call for the confiscation of all public-owned firearms, even though the vast majority of firearm owners are law-abiding citizens. Criminals do not conform to the law; therefore, banning the public ownership of firearms will not make any effort in reducing criminal activity of any kind. While many people are naïve to the potential reality of the confiscation of legally owned firearms, the possibility of this action is very real. Just as in Venezuela, publicly owned firearms are a threat to the full takeover of socialism in the United States.

Many of the current and former presidential candidates for the 2020 presidential election in the United States have repeatedly called and pushed for a series of measures in support of their efforts to restrict and eliminate the firearms owned by law-abiding citizens. One of these steps is a national gun registry.

A national gun registry is not only unnecessary, but dangerous to the constitutional freedoms of the American people. Legally purchased firearms are documented by the seller when they are purchased. There is no need or justification for a secondary registration of firearms, and state governments who have enacted such legislation have bypassed the Second Amendment and violated the constitutional rights of their citizens. The actual purpose of a national registry is to provide the socialist members of the United States government with the location of all publicly owned firearms in order to simplify the confiscation process. Remember, this practice was exercised in theory back in 1952.

Another concern regarding the increasing presence of socialism in the United States is the war against Christian beliefs and the practice of the Christian faith in America. At one time, America was considered a God-fearing nation. Sadly, this is no longer the case. The values of the upcoming generations are certainly not the same as those of their parents and grandparents. In addition, the gross disrespect many children today show towards their parents is another sign of the deterioration of American society. Unfortunately, this attitude of disrespect is fueled by the teachings of secular educators who have instilled in parents a fear of disciplining their children.

A growing trait in America is the lack of any sense of responsibility or accountability for one's actions. All people have a free will, but as far back as creation, we are shown that free will comes with a sense of responsibility, and there are consequences for misuse and/or abuse of that responsibility. Laws, rules, and regulations have existed in human culture for centuries with the purpose of maintaining order in society and promoting safety.

For example, many states have passed laws prohibiting texting and driving. These laws were passed for the protection of the public, but they are violated by hundreds of thousands of drivers each day. In 2015, a seventeen-year-old female was driving a pickup truck in Minnesota with three other teenage passengers. The driver was continuously texting on her cell phone while driving, and one of her passengers repeatedly asked her to stop texting at least eight times only to receive angry and profane rebukes from the driver. Allegedly, the driver stated she did not care if she crashed. A few moments later, the texting driver of the pickup truck ran a red light and crashed into another vehicle, killing two people, including a ten-year-old girl. In addition, two other children riding in the vehicle were injured. All the occupants of the pickup truck were injured but survived the crash. The seventeen-year-old driver of the pickup truck was eventually charged with multiple counts of vehicular homicide; however, she only received community service.

Many of socialism's proponents have openly argued for the abolishment of prisons, the expungement of convictions for certain crimes, and the restrictions on American's law enforcement agencies, and, over the years, the Socialist Party U.S.A. has stated clearly its goals and demands for American society in relation to law enforcement and criminal justice.

One of the Socialist Party U.S.A's demands is the immediate release of what it dubs non-violent offenders. Non-violent crime is still a crime with perpetrators and victims. Each time a person burns down a house or business with the intention of collecting the insurance money, a crime commonly known as insurance fraud, every citizen who is a client of the insurance company involved is a victim in the form of increased premiums, along with the company which has been defrauded of thousands of dollars. Whenever a person shoplifts from the local department store, the public pays the price in the form of increased prices. The list is endless. The point is laws are established for public safety and maintaining order in society. When laws are broken, there must be an accountability; otherwise, the law serves no purpose and good order in society is lost.

Socialists, for some reason, do not seem to believe in personal accountability for one's actions unless the action is an obstacle to or in disagreement with the Socialist Party. Then such accountability is screamed for and demanded. Socialists condone mandatory minimum sentences. What they fail to understand is the failure to hold people accountable for criminal acts encourages criminal acts. A criminal who is not held accountable and firmly punished will continue to commit crimes, and the nature of those crimes will tend to grow in severity.

George Kelly, also known as "Machine Gun Kelly," a college-educated man, started out dealing in untaxed liquor. He later expanded his endeavors into armed bank robbery and, finally, kidnapping. Regardless of what psychologists and psychiatrists believe or profess, small-time criminals will sooner or later become hardened criminals unless something is done to deter them from continuing down the road of lawlessness.

Felony criminal conviction carries with it the loss of certain privileges. One of these is voting rights. However, socialists continue to push for the restoration of voting rights for convicted felons who have completed their prison sentence. While the conduct of good post-incarceration behavior should indeed allow an individual to regain certain privileges which their crimes have required them to forfeit, there should be a lengthy period of trial under supervision during which an individual must prove to both the authorities and the public they have truly been reformed and have earned the reestablishment of their voting privileges.

Socialists also have called for rights of prisoners to organize unions to make demands on the administrators of the facilities where they are incarcerated. A prison where the prisoners run the prison is a disaster waiting for a chance to happen.

Several years ago, the inmates of a large municipal jail located in Virginia began to file complaints against the sheriff about their so-called rights to access to cable television. The sheriff agreed to investigate the matter; however, the end result was not what the inmates expected.

After thoroughly researching the requirements, the sheriff informed the inmates that he was indeed required to provide them with access to cable television, but according to established legislation, he was only required to provide them with two channels, and it was in his power to determine which channels would be provided. After informing the inmates that if their complaints continued they would be provided with the Weather Channel and the Cooking Channel, all complaints from the inmates ceased.

When the Federal Penitentiary at Alcatraz was opened in 1934 it was not intended to make good citizens. Rather, it was established to make good inmates. The problems of violence, gang activity, instigations of revolt against authority, and other issues plagued correctional facilities in the 1930s. Hardcore criminals apprehended by federal, state, and local authorities began to cause chaos in the nation's correctional facilities and interfere with the futures of other inmates who a genuine opportunity of rehabilitation and reintroduction to society. The Federal Bureau of Prisons, as a solution to this problem, came up with the idea of placing all the troublemakers in one prison. Convicted prisoners who were transferred to Alcatraz from the Federal Penitentiary's at Atlanta, Georgia, and Fort Leavenworth, Kansas, found their new home to be somewhat less accommodating than previous facilities. Prisoners at Alcatraz were informed they were entitled to food, clothing, a place to sleep, and basic medical care. Anything else was a privilege which could be revoked at the slightest infraction of the most menial rule.

In 1948, in one of the boldest escape attempts in the prison's history, a group of inmates managed to gain access to the security catwalk located on one end of the main cell house and seized a bolt action rifle, a handgun, and several rounds of ammunition. Their efforts to exit the cell house were foiled by the quick thinking of an injured guard who was taken hostage but managed to dispose of the one key which would have given the inmates a means to escape from the main cell house. Once their plan was ruined, the inmates called the warden of Alcatraz, James Johnston, and attempted to discuss a deal. Warden Johnston informed them the only possible deal was to throw out their weapons and surrender. With their limited armament, three of the main inmates involved in the plot attempted to make a stand against the correctional officers who were attempting to regain control of the prison. Their resistance was met with small arms fire and explosives. Some news agencies from San Francisco allegedly expressed concerned over "innocent prisoners" being injured, to which Warden Johnston supposedly reminded them that there were no innocent prisoners in Alcatraz.

Prisons, despite their negative image, serve an important role in America; they keep those who have no regard for the law from being a threat and impact on the rest of society. Whether a convicted individual is a violent or non-violent offender, they are still guilty of violating the law which was established to maintain public order and safety.

In addition, socialists have voiced their demands for organizations to openly interfere with law enforcement officers and agencies in the performance of their duties, with the ultimate elimination of police agencies. In 2019, Governor Gavin Newsom of California signed Assembly Bill 392 into law. Assembly Bill 392 states a law enforcement officer may use deadly force only when necessary to defend against an imminent threat of death or serious injury to officers or bystanders. What Governor Newsom fails to grasp is that officers have often been injured while trying to take combative and resistive criminal suspects into custody. No true and sincere officer of the law ever desires to take the life of another, and in departments across the nation, this is already established policy. The problem is Governor Newsom has gravely restricted the ability of law enforcement officers to judge what an imminent threat is or is not.

Law enforcement academies and associated training programs teach and train officers on a concept known as "minimum safe distance." Minimum safe distance is the space an officer attempts to maintain between the officer and a suspect who is displaying threatening or questionable behavior. A criminal suspect can kill with or without a firearm. Over the years, law enforcement officers have been run over with vehicles, stabbed with knives, struck with blunt objects, blinded with chemicals, and killed or injured by countless other attacks which do not involve firearms including a criminal who attacks barehanded.

Suspects who have their hands concealed when confronted are especially dangerous. Those concealed hands may contain nothing, or they may contain a knife, a gun, or even some type of chemical spray. Officers who are confronted by suspects with concealed hands are at a severe disadvantage and must make split second decisions which could have severe effects on themselves or innocent bystanders. If an officer hesitates, either through indecision or through fear of retribution, to react decisively against an assailant who may not be displaying a visible weapon, the result could be death or serious injury to the officer and others.

Between 2014 and 2018, 745 law enforcement officers fell in the line of duty. Of these, 245 were killed by gunfire, 246 died in vehicle crashes or were struck by vehicles in the performance of their duties, and 254 died from other causes.

By mid-2020, ninety-four law enforcement officers had killed in the line of duty over the course of barely six months. This number represents an increase of law enforcement officers of 49 percent, and of those, twenty-two had been shot. The majority of these and all other fallen law enforcement officers had families and left behind wives, husbands, and children. But to socialists, these lives and the lives of their loved ones who were left behind appear to be irrelevant.

Governor Newsom and all of those who supported Assembly Bill 392 should consider the fact that the assured hesitation to act which they have thrust into the minds of California's law enforcement officers in a sense makes them responsible for any California officer who is injured or killed in the future by some suspect who was able to keep a weapon concealed long enough to use it against a responding officer.

On countless occasions, the public has rushed to the assistance of a law enforcement officer who is engaged in a struggle to apprehend a suspect and who has been injured or incapacitated in the process. In a further attempt to hamstring the law enforcement officers of the state of California, Governor Newsom also signed into effect a law which absolves the public of the legal responsibility to assist a law enforcement officer upon his or her request. Apparently, Governor Newsom would rather see the law enforcement officers of California injured or killed than receive help from the public which they strive to protect.

One of Socialism's obstacles is an older and middle-aged generation who sees through the cloud of socialist's deceptive enticements and messages. Since they find it more difficult to sway this group of America's citizens, socialists instead focus their efforts on an easier target: the younger generation and children. In order to accomplish this, socialists have, over the years, been carefully and covertly cultivating a system of nationalized education.

Nationalized education, incorporated into the nation's kindergarten through twelfth grade education system, is rapidly becoming an indoctrination system rather than an educational system. Many parents tragically are so wrapped up in their busy schedules they are not even aware of what their children are being taught and, at times, forced to accept in school. Some schools have gone to great lengths to undermine the religious beliefs of families and have forced certain religious teachings on children regardless of their personal beliefs. In addition, socialists have expressed their desire for complete funding for public education while at the same time demanding the elimination of public funding and support for religious, private, and charter schools. This should not be surprising as these educational institutions typically do not promote pro-socialist indoctrination and agendas. Socialists have expressed several demands and desires regarding education in the United States, most of which are impractical or impossible to support. While their demands may indeed possess some positive attributes, they are financially, organizationally, and administratively impossible to achieve. In addition, socialists have no realistic plans for how to pay for the educational services they have called for.

Another interesting demand made by socialists is the removal of all law enforcement officers and/or security personnel from schools hosting elementary through high school age children. Not only is this idea dangerous, it is ludicrous. Tragically, in a day and age where individuals elect to deal with their personal problems by inflicting pain and suffering on others, a law enforcement presence in schools has become a necessity. School law enforcement and resource officers serve numerous roles including protecting the staff and students from both internal and external threats, enforcing school zone traffic laws, controlling traffic at school crossings during student arrival and dismissal, and doing everything within their power to intercept potential problems and threats before they have the opportunity to become a tragic reality.

In May of 2018, an alert school resource officer was able to intervene and prevent a potential mass shooting at a high school in Dixon, Illinois. On March 21, 2018 an alert school resource officer's rapid intervention stopped a school shooting at Great Mills High School in Maryland. In another 2018 incident, a school resource officer was able to advert a potential disaster by stopping an armed aggressor at Forest High School in Ocala, Florida, within a matter of minutes. Many other incidents have been thwarted by alert school officers, students, and staff who have identified potential threats through overheard comments, individual actions, and social media and taken immediate steps to neutralize potential threats before they have a chance to manifest themselves.

Despite what many individuals think, no system, no person, no resource is perfect. But dedicated law enforcement personnel are a critical component in school safety and crisis prevention, despite what socialists believe and profess.

The socialist goal of elimination of the concept of private ownership of property and businesses is being manifested in the growing efforts among socialists in the United States to create and keep in place a nationalized healthcare system. Such a system would set the United States government solely in charge of a citizen's well-being and health care. Nationalized health care is sold to the public on the platform of "healthcare for everyone." But what it has proven to evolve into time and time again is a system that leaves many individuals waiting for long periods of time for healthcare and fails to attract physicians and other medical professionals because the system does not properly compensate them for their efforts.

In short, the socialist agenda involves the creation of a secular society in which freedom is suppressed, Christian-based faith is oppressed, laziness and drug use is encouraged and excused, and there are no standards of law and order except as desired by those in power for their own personal benefit. Socialists demand the ultimate provision for everyone's wants with no accountability for one's actions or lack thereof. The end result is a society and culture which eventually degrades into an unsustainable quagmire of chaos and misery from which there is little hope of escape.

Individuals who have successfully managed to escape from socialist countries have openly stated that the socialist governments they once lived under only served to destroy businesses, destroy equality, increase taxes until no one can pay them, steal and redistribute land and property in the name of social justice, increase poverty, destroy the quality of healthcare, induce hunger and starvation, abolish parental rights in the education of their children, abolish the freedom to practice one's faith in accordance with their beliefs, and drive countless citizens out of nations into a refugee status.

The concept of socialism has repeatedly shown itself to be a recurrent failure, never delivering what it promises and accomplishing nothing except for oppressing freedoms and destroying lives. Socialist governments around the world have collapsed one after the other, yet the serpent continues to rear its head in new areas and among new cultures populated with increasing numbers of naïve and uninformed citizens who are enticed to embrace the idol of socialism without ever making an effort to find out what it truly represents and endeavors to accomplish. The modern and self-centered generation which is migrating from adolescence adulthood is blindly falling for the deception of socialism at an ever-increasing rate. Unless the up and coming leaders of America open their eyes to the truth of the danger which lurks just beyond the horizon, the United States of America, which has stood as a free and independent nation for nearly two-and-a-half centuries, will slowly but surely cease to exist.

CHAPTER NINE

THE IMMINENT THREAT

As the United States of America moves toward the latter part of the first quarter of the twenty-first century, the message of Socialism is being increasingly preached at and thrust upon the American people. Through socialist-minded professors in the nation's institutions of higher learning, the future generations are being programed to embrace socialist ideology without fully understanding what it truly entails. Political leaders who are openly and adamantly socialists are being elected to office by an increasingly naïve and unwary population with no memory of the tragedies of the past and little concern for the coming tragedies of the future. Their efforts are being strongly assisted by another organization which has made considerable effort to promote socialists and socialism while slandering and attacking the characters of its opponents. That organization is the News Media.

Just as the Soviets used the radio stations of captured territories to spread their propaganda in the closing days of the Second World War, the modern news media in the United States has increasingly displayed a tendency to air favorable and frequent broadcasts of socialists and their message while ignoring or blatantly silencing the voices of socialism's opponents. Rather than reporting news events without bias, over the past several years, the modern news media in the United States has clearly expressed favoritism toward liberal and socialist proponents and activists, and often reports only one side of a story without sharing all of the facts involved in newsworthy events.

In addition, the growing complacency of upcoming generations has served as a catalyst and a channel for socialism to gain a stronger foothold among the American population. Far too many people are completely oblivious to the looming disaster which is hanging like guillotine blade over this nation. Where socialism had all but disappeared from American culture in the 1950s, it has recently began a resurgence due to its proponents using the news media, social media, institutions of higher learning, and any other means at their disposal to proclaim their message to anyone who will listen as to all the things which are supposedly wrong with our current government and ideology.

Socialists are probably the most pessimistic people in society. They cry out repeatedly about the impending disaster of climate issues, social issues, economic issues, and any other issue they can identify or invent. Socialists tend to only view and emphasize the negative aspects of society and declare their system will right the wrongs of the current situation. They aggressively attack the characters, families, institutions, and ideas of those who oppose them and continue their attacks relentlessly regardless of whether their accusations have merit or not. Socialists also tend to base their arguments on inaccurate or fabricated data and information.

For example, socialist proponents consistently condemn the financially successful and blame them for the struggling lives of others. Often referred to as social or economic inequality, the facts of the situation present a different picture than that painted by socialist.

Between 2005 and 2015, statistics indicate income inequality in the United States actually decreased, and by 2017, the general household income actually increased by 10 percent. In addition, the socialist perception that unemployment is a crisis has also proven to be inaccurate. Over a twelve-year period, the ration of traditional full-time employees for individuals between the ages of twenty-five to fifty-four increased from 89:100 in 2005 to 97:100 in 2017, but socialists continue to scream about the crisis of unemployment and blame their opponents for the so-called problem.

One of the emerging dangers of socialism lies in the deceptive titles worn by several recent socialists who have risen to various positions of power in government. The most recent such title is carried by several individuals who refer to themselves as "democratic socialists." The title alone is a deception because there is nothing democratic about socialism. Socialists promise to provide all kinds of services and privileges for those of lower incomes by slapping horrendous taxes on those who have worked with vigor and labored with commitment to achieve their status and earn their compensation. Socialists literally view certain individual's financial success as a crime and justify taking money, land, and other resources from those who are successful and turning it over to individuals who do not display any desire of put forth any effort to work or better themselves.

Of course, the crime of being financially successful does not apply to socialists or socialist sympathetic individuals. Consider the following information:

Name	Approximate Net Worth
Joe Biden	$1.5 Million Dollars (The Street)
Bernie Sanders	$2.5 Million Dollars (Forbes)
Elizabeth Warren	$12 Million Dollars (Forbes)
Nancy Pelosi	$120 Million Dollars (Celebrity Net Worth)
Charles Schumer	$900 Thousand Dollars (Celebrity Net Worth)
Diane Feinstein	$80 Million Dollars (Celebrity Net Worth)
Beto O'Rourke	$4 Million Dollars (Forbes)

……. just to name a few.

Another concern regarding socialist ideology involves their efforts to hold certain businesses legally liable for the misuse of their products. However, this effort by socialist proponents only seems to be levied at the firearms industry. Many socialist proponents have advocated for allowing firearms manufacturers to be held liable when their products are used in violent criminal acts. Not only is this ideology unjustified, it is hypocritical.

According to the Institute of Insurance Safety, a total of 35,092 people were killed in automobile accidents in 2015. It is interesting that no recommendations have been made by socialists to hold vehicle manufacturers liable for deaths caused by their products. Liberty Mutual Research Institute for Safety stated in 2007 approximately four hundred individuals suffered fatal injuries as a result of falling from ladders or scaffolding, but no calls have been voiced by socialists for holding the manufacturers of ladders or scaffolding liable for these deaths.

Ladders, like automobiles and firearms, are simply tools. Using tools requires human responsibility to ensure their safe and proper operation. Vehicles do not simply start themselves and drive off down a street with the intention of killing or injuring someone any more than ladders make the decision to topple. Neither to firearms intentionally of their own free will set out to injure nor kill people. There must be an individual behind the instrument to create an action.

For example, fatal traffic accidents due to excessive speeding kill over thirty thousand people each year. Driving a motor vehicle at excessive or irresponsible speeds, failure to obey traffic control devices (red lights, stop signs, etc.), improper passing, and improper lane usage is a personal choice. Drivers who repeatedly refuse to obey traffic laws eventually cause traffic accidents, and certain violations may result in the revocation of an individual's driving privileges. In addition, over the past decade, over 113,000 people were killed in traffic accidents which were related to an individual or individuals driving under the influence of alcohol or a controlled substance. Again, a vehicle cannot physically force a person who is under the influence to enter that vehicle, turn on the ignition, place the vehicle in drive, and proceed down the roadway. An individual makes the decision, and it is the individual who must and should be held accountable.

In 2017, the population of the United States was estimated at nearly 327,000,000 people. Of that estimated population, some 2,813,503 people died over the course of that same year. Of those individuals, approximately 40,000 individuals were killed in motor vehicle accidents; some 5,100 individuals were killed in industrial accidents; 647,457 died of heart disease; 599,108 succumbed to cancer; 169,936 died in general accidents; approximately 160,201 perished due to chronic lower respiratory diseases; 146,383 died due to suffering a stroke; approximately 121,404 died of Alzheimer's disease; nearly 83,564 died from diabetes; about 55,672 from influenza and pneumonia; nephritis, nephrotic syndrome, and nephrosis claimed some 50,633 lives; and there were approximately 47,173 suicides. That same year, approximately 39,773 individuals were killed by firearms, and of those, approximately 60 percent were suicide related. These deaths constituted approximately .01 percent of the total deaths which occurred in the United States over the course of 2017, yet the law-abiding citizens who own firearms in the United States have come under increasing attacks by socialist proponents over the past several years.

Why? Because unlike disease, traffic accidents, and so forth, firearms owners stand in the way of a socialist takeover of the United States. History has proven repeatedly when governments restrict or abolish firearm ownership, the end result is tyranny. Put simply, an unarmed population is an unsafe population.

Over the course of the twentieth century, tyrannical governments have murdered up to four times as many of their own people than those who lost their lives in all the armed conflicts occurring around the world during the same period of time. On the same note, history has shown that in countries where firearm ownership was restricted or abolished, the governments of those nations were responsible for killing more citizens than criminals were.

For example, between 1914 and 1923, in what is now modern day Turkey, the Ottoman Empire slaughtered some 1.5 million Armenians; following the Soviet Union's implementation of gun control in 1929, the government killed over twenty million so-called dissidents over a period of twenty years; by the end of 1938, some twenty million individuals who resisted the government of Communist China lost their lives at the hands of government authorities after gun control laws had been set into place approximately seventeen years earlier; in 1938, Nazi Germany set gun control laws in place specifically in regards to Jews, and by the end of World War Two, Hitler's government had murdered over six million Jews along with many who tried to protect them; officials in Cambodia killed approximately one million people by 1956, barely two years after gun control laws were placed into effect; approximately one hundred thousand Mayan Indians were slain in Guatemala over a nine-year period after gun control laws were enacted in 1964; over three hundred thousand Christians were slaughtered by the Ugandan Government after gun control laws were placed into effect in 1970; and after disarming the Tutsi people in 1994, the government of Rwanda executed nearly one million members of that tribe.

The tragic reality is many of the up and coming generations who will be the future leaders of this country are oblivious to such concerns and are instead blindsided by socialist propaganda. Many Americans of the young adult generation are leaning toward supporting liberal and socialist platforms rather than the conservative viewpoints of their parents and grandparents. When Franklin Delano Roosevelt accepted the Democratic nomination for president in 1936, he stated, *"There is a mysterious cycle in human events. To some generations much is given. Of others much is expected. This generation of Americans has a rendezvous with destiny."* (F.D. Roosevelt, 1936) The question lying before the nation as we move deeper into the twenty-first century is what will that destiny be?

In the aftermath of the surprise attack on the US Pacific Fleet at Pearl Harbor, Americans of all races and creeds rallied to the cause of defending their nation against outside aggression. White, Black, Asian, and American Indian, rich and poor, famous and unknown served side-by-side, putting aside their differences and disagreements as they endeavored to pursue a common goal: defeating the enemy and protecting America. All these individuals fought under the same flag: the flag of the United States of America; a symbol of freedom which was once revered and respected by all is now desecrated by many of its nation's citizens.

In 1989, the United States Supreme Court, in a disturbing decision, ruled that the burning of the American flag was an action protected under the First Amendment. In a 5 – 4 vote in the case of *Texas v. Johnson (1989)*, with Associate Justices William Brennan, Anthony Kennedy, Thurgood Marshall, Harry Blackmun, and Antonin Scalia voting in favor of the decision, and Chief Justice William Rehnquist and Associate Justices John Paul Stevens, Sandra Day O'Connor, and Byron White dissenting, ruled in favor of Gregory Lee Johnson, an activist affiliated with the Revolutionary Communist Party U.S.A. in his appeal after being arrested for burning the American flag. That same flag which has draped the coffins of fallen men and women of all races: White, Black, Hispanic, Asian, American Indian, and others.

In today's day and age, younger generations of Americans burn and desecrate the American flag in the name of free speech. Children were once cherished and protected in our nation, but today many of America's leaders, along with young to middle-aged adults and others, are screaming for the unborn to be slaughtered in great big bloody batches. A reverence for God is slowly being replaced by a reverence for personal opinion, whether good or bad. Respect for one's elders, parents, law enforcement officers, teachers, pastors, and neighbors has gone out the window. And self-discipline is rapidly becoming a thing of the past. More and more members of the up and coming generations no longer believe in any sense of accountability for their actions or the actions of others.

The attitude of many of the younger generation of Americans has been reflected in their choice of national leadership. Several national polls taken in the second half of 2019 suggests approximately 70 percent of younger voters between the ages of twenty-three and thirty-eight would cast their ballot for a socialist candidate. Tragically, practically none of those who are embracing socialism have any idea of its consequences. Why would young American voters become so anxious to embrace an ideology which ultimately destroys freedoms and abolishes what the founding fathers of this nation referred to as inalienable rights? The answer may lie in a growing assessment of millennials as an "entitled generation."

During the period of the 1980s, current millennials were still babies or were not yet even born. It was during this period of time that many large corporations and large banks became common. Certain large businesses were critical to the status of the nation's economy, and the failure of such businesses had the potential to create economic disaster. As a result, the banks needed special assistance from the government to avoid a national catastrophe.

During 2007 and 2008, the economy in the United States suffered a downturn and those belonging to the millennial group witnessed many tragic events: their parents lost jobs, homes, savings, and became burdened with excessive debt, and at the same time, many average citizens were suffering, large banks and corporations were receiving bail-outs from the government. This undoubtably led an increasing number of millennials to consider the idea the economic beliefs of their parents and grandparents were ineffective or outdated.

The chain reaction of events which stemmed from the economic crisis which emerged during the 2007/2008 time period brought about many difficult decisions: older Americans elected to wait on retirement and continue working. This filled jobs which millennials hoped to step into. Education became increasingly expensive, and millennials found themselves burdened in financial debt in their efforts to secure the training and education which they hoped would qualify them for jobs and careers. Facing the reality of lower incomes from being forced to accept lower paying jobs, many millennials continued to live with their parents, elected to wait on marriage and/or starting their own families, and invest in other major endeavors such as buying a home.

In addition, millennials "want things" like anyone else, but instead of working and saving for cars, homes, and other items of desire, millennials have been lured into the deceptive trap of the credit card. Charge now and pay later. Unfortunately, instead of credit card use helping many millennials, it has chained them with a mountain of debt which becomes ever increasingly difficult to erase, and to these younger Americans, the "Robin Hood" message of taking from the rich and giving to the poor is very appealing. Why endeavor to work hard and strive to better oneself if potentially future political leaders are willing to give individuals rewards instead of requiring that they work for them and earn them?

Millennials came into the world as the turbulent years of the Cold War were fading into history. Practically none of them have any concept of the pain and suffering inflicted upon millions of people in numerous countries by the hard and cold forces of socialism and communism. Despite the education millennials have received, their education has been craftily censored by liberal and socialist-minded educators and educational institutions so that millennials have no idea how serious a threat to their own future socialism truly is.

It is not difficult to understand how millennials could fall for such a deception. Many people today choose to simply accept what they are told or taught without looking into the facts. Millennials are so caught up in the day-to-day grind of trying to scrape out a meager living they have little or no interest in using their free time to investigate what is broadcast to them on the news networks or preached to them by liberal and socialist-sympathetic politicians. The current economic situation is viewed by many millennials as hindering and oppressing their upward movement in life, and this way of thinking makes them prime targets for the proponents of socialism who are luring their victims into their web with the deceptive message of a kinder-gentler, more-giving and less-taking concept of socialism. Tragically, millennials are falling for this lie in increasing numbers and are failing to listen to the warnings of their parents and grandparents.

Another factor which is affecting the way younger generations of Americans think is rooted in a complacent interest in the teachings of history, or the lack thereof. Many of America's institutions of higher learning are teaching twisted and warped versions of history rather than discussing actual facts. American history is not always pretty, but facts are facts, and when the truth is examined and contemplated, valuable lessons may be learned as to how to deal with similar issues in the future. Instead of focusing on teaching history as it happened, a growing number of educators care more about the situations of the present than they do about the lessons of the past.

The fact is that threats from the past are alive and well in the present day. They roam about in new disguises but deceive with the same messages. The proponents of socialism use the same tactics to sway their audiences that their predecessors did. They create an enemy, find a point of blame, and then launch into a message of how evil and ineffective their opponents are while praising and promoting their own views and ideas. They invent crises and injustices, and they invent ways to link their opponents and things they disagree with to those crises and injustices. They brand their opponents as the enemies of all and proclaim the wonderful solutions and benefits which are at the fingertips of voters…if they will just give them their support. The nation of Germany did just that, succumbing to the tempting message of Adolf Hitler who blamed an entire race of people for Germany's problems, enticed the citizens to give him their support, and then led the nation down the road to destruction.

America's millennials today are falling for the same deceptive message that the German people did over eighty years ago. The faces have changed, the tactics are more cloaked in disguise, but the threat is the same. A growing number of current and potential leaders in the United States are either open or closet proponents of socialism and all that it truly stands for. One of the most vocal of modern-day socialist in America is Senator Bernie Sanders from the state of Vermont.

Sanders presents himself as a Democratic Socialist. This is an interesting title being that true democracy and socialism can never exist side-by-side. In an article published in 2015, Bernie Sanders made several points about his concept of socialism, one of which was the following: "*Human beings have the right to control their own lives.*" (Sanders, 2015) Sanders has also made a strong push for abortion under the message of freedom of choice.

In an article published in February of 2015, Sanders made a push for his Medicare-For-All Single-Payer program. Despite a Gallup poll which revealed 70 percent of those who obtain health care through their employer's desire to hold on to that coverage, Sanders couldn't care less. When asked by CNN anchor Wolf Blitzer if those individuals would be able to keep their private insurance plans, Sanders replied emphatically: "*No.*" In addition, former presidential candidate Kamala Harris of California stated in January of 2015 her plan for eliminating private health insurance. So much for the freedom of choice. From the socialist point of view, freedom of choice only applies if a person chooses what is acceptable to the socialists who are in power.

But despite socialism's growing acceptance among younger Americans, there is still a large percentage of the American population who have not fallen victim to socialism's deceptive message. In an article published in The Hill, a Monmouth University Poll revealed that the majority of Americans (57 percent) believe socialism is not compatible with American values and only 10 percent of American's polled have a positive view of socialism. However, the same poll also revealed that 45 percent of Americans maintained a neutral status on the issue, and it is in that 45 percent that the danger to America's future lies.

On the issue of gun control, a matter emphatically pursued by many current socialist proponents, Bernie Sanders implied that he believed most gun owners would never commit an act of violence with a firearm. However, at the same time, he suggested that law-abiding gun owners should make "concessions." It is in those concessions where the deception of socialism so effectively hides.

Due to the fact that many gun owners possess more than one legally owned firearm, it is impossible to calculate an exact number of gun owners in the United States. According to the 2017 census, the population of the United States totaled approximately 315,000,000 people. Over the course of the 2017 year, approximately 1,247,321 violent crimes were committed in the United States, according to statistics compiled by the FBI. Of those crimes committed, approximately 17,284 were homicides. Statistics vary depending on the source consulted; however, the numerical picture is fairly clear.

Other studies reveal that of the approximate gun-related deaths reported in 2017, approximately six out of ten were related to suicides. With an approximate number of gun-owners in the United States numbering approximately 190 million, the numbers roughly indicate that, in 2017, the number of violent crimes in the United States were committed by roughly three percent of the total population. Yet socialists and their supporters are adamantly attacking the majority of the American population which consists of law-abiding citizens!

Ultimately, the safety of the American public is not the primary goal of socialists and their advocates. Their message of combating gun-related violence is a front for a more ominous goal: disarming the law-abiding American population for the purpose of removing the most serious obstacle to a socialist takeover of the United States. Even though the Founding Fathers who penned our Constitution died over two centuries ago, their foresight in including and requiring the Second Amendment as a requirement for the ratification of the Constitution is commendable. It because of the threats facing America today, including socialism, our Founding Fathers included the Second Amendment: the clear, concise, unamendable, and irrevocable right of the citizens to keep and bear arms, to the United States Constitution.

The growing tide of socialism in America should be an alarm for all to acknowledge. Unfortunately, this ideology is becoming increasingly rooted in American society and will continue to do so until the very structure and values which the United States is founded upon are broken apart and destroyed, and the unwary American population is increasingly oblivious to socialism's looming threat. By the time younger Americans are truly aware of what they have to lose in a Socialist America, the damage will be done, and it will be too late.

CHAPTER TEN

THE EVENTUAL OUTCOME
OF SOCIALISM IN AMERICA

Throughout human history, people have suffered poverty, injustice, and oppression. One self-professed savior after another has risen from the masses
proclaiming a message of deliverance in return for a people's acceptance of
and obedience to his or her leadership. The end result is always the same.

In the Bible, Cain killed Abel because Abel's values were accepted, and
Cain's were rejected. The Egyptians enslaved the Israelites because they saw
them as a threat, even though, according to the Bible, the Israelite Joseph,
through his gifts of organization and management, had saved the whole region
from starvation some two centuries earlier. The Philistines later gained a dis-
tinct advantage over the Israelites because they possessed superior weapons;
weapons the possession of which was forbidden to the Israelites. Feudal serfs
labored to serve their feudal masters, believing there was no other way of life
available, and the caste system in India held certain segments of the population
in poverty generation after generation because no other way of life was believed possible. The American Indians were presented with many promises
again and again, only to be repeatedly betrayed, eventually disarmed, and in
time, their culture was all but eradicated.

As stated earlier, history has a tendency to repeat itself. One reason for
this is that humanity is infected by the devastating trait of not learning from

past mistakes. During the twentieth century, most Americans would have cringed at the thoughts of a socialist-controlled government, but as we approach the later years of the first quarter of the twenty-first century, that concern is becoming a thing of the past.

In addition, many Americans are falling for the same deceptions used by socialist tyrants of the past without entertaining any question of what is at risk in their future. In truth, many of those Americans who are turning a curious ear to socialism or embracing it completely are oblivious to the fact that the freedoms they enjoy today are not compatible with socialism. That is because the concepts of socialism and freedom are not compatible. And the evidence of this is becoming crystal clear with each passing day.

Socialists and their sympathizers do not believe in listening to or abiding by the will of the masses, even when that will is protected under the guidelines of the United States Constitution. When it was created and set in place, our government structure was instilled with a system of checks and balances to prevent any one individual or any one group from obtaining and securing "absolute power." But if the United States Constitution is not supported and defended by those who swore a solemn oath to do so, then it becomes nothing more than a worthless piece of paper.

The recent Covid-19 pandemic has been exploited by many socialist and socialist-type leaders at the federal, state, and local levels of government in the United States in a frontline battle to ram socialism down the throats of the American people. One aspect of this effort is manifested in the actions of many state leaders who have either persuaded their state governments or demanded and received from their state legislatures' "emergency powers" to deal with the Covid-19 situation, and many of those state leaders have used their "emergency powers" to attack, restrict, or eliminate rights which are guaranteed and protected by the United States Constitution. This has led to many state governors obtaining what some historians in the past have referred to as "Absolute Power." And many governors have held onto that "absolute power," which they wrap up in the blanket of executive privilege like a prized toy, which they abhor idea of relinquishing.

For example, Governor Gretchen Whitmer of Michigan, extended the lockdown requirements, despite open opposition from both citizens and the Michigan State Legislature. Governors do have certain executive powers to take certain actions apart from the approval of the state's legislative body, but those powers are limited by state constitutions. Certain members of Michigan's legislature have pointed out that while the state legislature does have the authority to extend a declared state of emergency, the governor does not.

In another area of concern which has arisen during the recent Covid-19 concern, many state leaders have endeavored and, in some cases, succeeded in attacking the constitutional freedom and first amendment right of Freedom of Worship. Churches and church leaders around the country have been threatened, chastised, fined, and suffered other such actions at the command of their state leaders for standing up for this right.

In a recent example of suppression of the freedom of worship in America, California Governor Gavin Newsom issued an order restricting churches to allow only 25 percent of its congregational space to be utilized in order to permit in-house worship services. South Bay United Pentecostal church in Chula Vista, located in San Diego County, challenged Newson's actions. The case eventually made its way to the United States Supreme Court where the evidence of socialism's influence was clearly manifested by the actions of America's ultimate court authority which is charged with upholding the constitutionality of all approved legislation. Supreme Court Associate Justices Ruth Bader Ginsburg, Stephen Breyer, Elena Kagan, and Sonia Sotomayor voted to uphold Governor Newsom's actions, while Associate Justices Anthony M. Kennedy, Neil M. Gorsuch, Clarence Thomas, and Brett Kavanaugh opposed him. And, in what should be a surprising turn of events, the deciding vote to support Governor Newson's unconstitutional restrictions of the Freedom of Worship established by the First Amendment to the United States Constitution was cast by Chief Supreme Court Justice John Roberts Jr.

Interestingly enough, Governor Newson's so-called restrictions in the interest of public health do not apply to other groups, such as diners, hair salons and barber shops, supermarkets, restaurants, cannabis dispensaries, and numerous other types of businesses. Governor Newsom's legal team argued that the Supreme Court decision in the case of *Jacobson v. Massachusetts* gives states broad powers during a public health emergency and effectively supersedes typical protections for First Amendment activity, including the practice of one's religious faith. It would behoove the American people to remember the powerful and profound words of Lord Acton, *"Power tends to corrupt and absolute power corrupts completely."* (Lord Acton, 1887)

One of the greatest deceptions of all is the socialist propaganda message of "free stuff." Free education, free cell phones, free food, free housing, free medical care, free this and free that. The idea of earning one's way in the world, earning the possessions they own, and giving an honest day's work for an honest day's pay is becoming a memory. What the majority of those who embrace socialism fail to understand or accept is that in reality—nothing is free! Everything cost somebody something. What one person fails to pay for, another must pick up the tab. None of the so-called "free stuff" offered by socialist proponents is actually free. Rather, individuals who work for their money, are responsible with their money, save and properly manage their money, and have earned their money, eventually are forced to pay—with their money—for services and provisions for people who either fail or refuse to do so.

Granted there are segments of society who sincerely need and are deservingly justified in receiving some type of government assistance. But the fact is that many Americans are growing increasingly lazy, irresponsible, complacent, and inattentive to the reality of life. An increasing percentage of the younger generations of Americans are becoming self-centered and close-minded and believe the world owes them something. This attitude is only amplified by the socialist message that personal responsibilities and desires should be provided by the masses.

For example, birth control is a personal responsibility. If a couple does not desire to bring children into the world, either temporarily or permanently, it is their responsibility to take the necessary actions, obtain the necessary needs at their own expense, and to take responsibility for their own actions and decisions. It is not and should not be a burden of other citizens who work, earn, save, and manage their finances to foot the bill for someone who either does not or will not do the same.

A college education costs money, and granted, many college tuition costs are outrageously high. But regardless of the fact that socialism believes in free education, education is not free. Any individual who receives a free college education will do so at the expense of someone else.

Another deceptive fact about socialism is that socialist proponents offer incredible and wonderful sounding things to people—things which are expensive. But they never openly reveal an honest, sincere, logical, and reasonable proposal as to how their programs will be financed. There is an old saying that those who fail to plan, plan to fail. The proponents of socialism have never truly planned; hence the reason socialism has always failed. Yet even though socialism has repeatedly failed in every instance which it has been implemented, individuals continue to arise and sing praises to its deceptive message.

Another crafty tactic of socialist proponents is the drive to legalize marijuana. Many people today see marijuana as a harmless substance which has many benefits. The proven reality is that marijuana kills brain cells (cells which do not regenerate) and is also what is commonly referred to as a gateway drug, the use of which eventually leads to the addiction to harder and increasingly dangerous substances such as heroin, cocaine, and so forth. Numerous studies which have been conducted over the years have revealed that the majority of hardcore drug addicts started on their downward spiral of addiction with an initial experimentation with marijuana use. Offering the promise of legalization of marijuana is an appealing tactic of socialists to many members of American society who are totally oblivious to its dangers.

Secretly, socialists probably enjoy the idea of an American culture and society blinded by the haze of marijuana-induced euphoria because a brain-dead culture is less likely to identify and resist their efforts to gain total control over American society.

In practically every nation where socialism's dark embrace has seized control of a population, its grip came on slowly and craftily, and by the time the people realized what was happening, the damage was done, and it was too late. A question one might pose as to how socialism could ever gain control in America? To answer that question, it is necessary to examine the steps which socialist proponents are already attempting to take.

First and foremost, the American population would have to be disarmed. An armed American population is an obstacle to socialism's advancement. Such a disarmament would be a direct violation of the Second Amendment to the Constitution of the United States and an overt act of treason. How could such a seemingly impossible endeavor be achieved?

First, gun buy-back programs (funded by the taxpayers) are currently being used to remove firearms from the hands of American citizens. We'll give you a little money if you'll give us your guns. People desperate for cash fall victim to this deception every day.

Next, if socialist proponents are successful in gaining enough power and influence in American government, a national gun registry would be implemented. The lack of such a registry is an important protection for law-abiding gun owners who make up the majority of the American population. With the implementation of a national registry, a socialist-controlled government would have a firm knowledge of the location of a vast majority of legally owned firearms; therefore, they would know where to go to confiscate them. When gun buy-back programs lose their effectiveness, the socialist leaders in America would then initiate orders for the so-called authorities to begin door-to-door confiscation of firearms in violation of the Second Amendment, and while many law enforcement agencies around the nation have openly voiced their refusal to comply with such activity, they in turn would be opening themselves up to attacks by socialist proponents.

Socialists and their closet supporters have and are now in the process of making powerful attempts to disarm the American population and have been hard at work at this endeavor for years. The message of so-called gun control, preached in the aftermath of tragic gun-related violence, is being increasingly embraced by individuals who are completely ignorant of the facts.

In April of 2020, Virginia Gov. Ralph Northam signed new legislation into law, launching an all-out attack on the First Amendment rights of law-abiding citizens. While he failed to achieve certain elements of his agenda, the damage was done with the stroke of a pen, and while some of Governor Northam's legislation was wrapped up in the guise of promoting public safety, the overall agenda is much darker. Governor Northam implied in his comments following the signing of his gun control legislation that he was not finished and would continue in his efforts which will most likely go even further at curtailing the Second Amendment rights of the people of Virginia.

Socialist proponents continue to attack the Second Amendment rights of America's citizens in the so-called name of public safety, but no proposed legislation in any state carries any weight in combating criminal activity. Criminals do not care about or abide by the law, and no amount of legislation will prevent future tragedies. Criminals will commit crimes regardless of any laws which are on the books. The true victims of gun-control legislation are law-abiding American citizens.

A gun, like a vehicle, does not act of its own accord. It is an inanimate object which requires the intent and action of an individual to produce the tragic outcomes which have repeatedly shattered so many lives around the nation. It should be clearly understood that gun-related violence, either against one individual or a multitude of individuals, is a hateful, unlawful, and irresponsible action and must be dealt with accordingly if there is to be any justice and a system of accountability in American society. But the gun itself is not the problem. The problem lies in the individual who pulls the trigger, and that same problem is compounded by the deteriorating values of American Society as increasing numbers of individuals succumb to the message of secular humanism, liberalism, and socialism.

In addition, as mentioned earlier, none of the legislation proposed and pushed by legislators at the federal, state, and local levels of government promises any impact against criminals. The only individuals affected by the legislation proposed by socialist and socialist sympathetic government officials are the law-abiding citizens of the United States of America whose ability to defend themselves against criminal activity both in their homes and on the streets will be increasingly reduced.

Once the American public is disarmed, the next step in a total socialist takeover would be the invalidation of certain elements of the United States Constitution, specifically the freedom of speech, the right to keep and bear arms, the freedom of peaceful assembly, the freedom of due process, and the freedom of religion, specifically in relation to Christianity. All these freedoms are a direct threat to the concept of socialism. It is important to remember and understand that the first ten amendments to the United States Constitution are not amendable or revocable. To do so would be an act of treason.

One question yet to be answered is this: would the United States military, after taking an oath to support and defend the Constitution of the United States against all enemies both foreign and domestic, take overt oppressive action against the American citizens whose freedoms are established and protected by that same Constitution? The next target of attack in socialist domination, which has already been underway for decades, involves an assault on the core of American society itself.

The central core of American society and culture is the family. The concept of the family was established by Almighty God in the Garden of Eden centuries ago in the form of one man (the husband), one woman (the wife), and, eventually, the product of their union: children. The husband and wife together shared the responsibility of raising and rearing their children in the divine values which they were given to live by and to initiate discipline when those rules were violated. Granted, humanity from the beginning was created with a free will, but with that free will come consequences for making the wrong choices. Through rearing and discipline, parents down through the ages have endeavored to prepare their children to make the right decisions and refrain from making the wrong ones.

During the second half of the twentieth century, Shafarevich's warning of the seeds of socialism destroying the central family unit became a growing reality. The rock of the traditional family structure has been eroded away over the past several decades with the legalization of abortion on demand, increasing divorce rates, and the establishment of government subsidized assistance for the growing numbers of single-parent families around the country. The growing number of government-sponsored assistance programs which socialist proponents claimed were critically important to support single-parent households required continually increasing taxes to fund them. A tragic reality is that the lives of many hardworking citizens have been devastated through the confiscation of personal property due to overbearing tax burdens. These programs have in turn created an attitude of trust in government and have drawn countless numbers of the American population away from the concept of faith in God. The government in a socialist-centered society sets up its own religion, values, and requirements.

Today, the concept of the family is being attacked, criticized, distorted, and endangered. The reference of an individual as "my wife," or "my husband," is being replaced with the terms, "my baby-daddy" or my "baby-mama." The increasing instability of the family home is being reflected in the attitudes and actions of the children coming out of such conditions.

Children who display no respect for their parents, their teachers, one another, or any form of authority, and who defy rules as if there are no consequences for doing so. The sad fact is that children today suffer little or no consequences for inappropriate behavior. Through the message and threats of liberal and socialist proponents and educators, parents have become terrified of disciplining their children out of fear of being subjected to legal action. Spare the rod and spoil the child. Unfortunately, such complacency produces children, adolescents, and young adults who come of age believing it is acceptable to violate the law and disrespect the rules of society, and the outcome is children still in their teens committing felony crimes which result in incarceration and other consequences before such a child even attains adulthood.

At the same time, the programing and lack of discipline of children through America's increasingly liberal and secular education system leads them to make tragic decisions which impact not only their lives, but the lives of others. Many children and adolescents today believe they are justified in dealing with their problems and issues with others through violence, aggression, and rebellion. Again and again, when a child or adolescent commits an act of violence, the excuse is raised that they were bullied. The fact is that two wrongs will never make a right, and in most cases, the bullied individual takes his or her anger out on those who they have no relationship or dealings with.

On the reverse side of the issue, children and adolescents feel justified in bullying others are oblivious through the lack of discipline and upbringing to the tragic impact of their actions on the lives of their victims. Even churches have become cold to the concept of the teaching: *love thy neighbor*.

In one tragic case which occurred during the early twentieth century, a young boy from an impoverished family, dressed in dirty clothes, approached a church in search of something positive to believe in. Unfortunately, he was turned away by church leaders. That young man, known as John Dillinger, grew up to become a violent, defiant, and ruthless criminal who robbed, killed, and terrorized the nation until his life was eventually taken in an act of violence which might have been avoided if the proper actions had been taken years earlier.

Over the course of the later twentieth century and the early years of the twenty-first century, the foundation has been laid for the ideology of socialism to take root and eventually take hold of American society. In a nation which was founded on the concept and love of freedom, how can this be possible? The answer is found in the slow and deceptive tactics of socialism's proponents.

In time, the iron grip of socialism threatens to become stronger and stronger until the precious freedoms enjoyed by American citizens for over two hundred years are only a distant memory. The education of America's children would no longer be a matter of parental consent or approval. Children would be indoctrinated (not educated) as to the goals, rules, and policies of socialism and discouraged from embracing the values instilled in them by the teachings of their parents, grandparents, and churches. Parental access to and freedom to challenge educational institutions would be suppressed if not ultimately eliminated.

The freedom of religion, specifically Christianity, would eventually be all but erased from American culture. As already mentioned, this freedom has been relentlessly attacked by many governors and other political figures in response to the recent Covid-19 virus issue. Using a demand for "social distancing" for the purpose of reducing the spread of the virus (a good cover story and partially justifiable), many state leaders arrogantly bypassed the First Amendment and all but outlawed worship services around the country, even to the point of threating so-called violators with fines or arrest.

Even in the so-called Bible Belt, this violation of the Constitution has reared its ugly head. One pastor in Mississippi was threatened by authorities for holding a "drive-in" worship service for Mother's Day utilizing an outdoor public address system and requiring worshippers to remain in their vehicles which were parked over six feet apart. These threats were totally unjustified, especially due to the fact that a drive-in restaurant located in the same area (with vehicle spacing being less than six feet) was allowed to continue with business as usual.

The leaders of state governments around the United States continue to oppress, threaten, and even target for legal action congregations and their leaders who elected to defy such tyrannical actions and stand up for their constitutional rights. It should be disturbing that so many state leaders have elected to give themselves such unbounded authority, which many are very reluctant to relinquish.

Socialism is a jealous god and allows no room for any allegiance to a Supreme Being other than itself. The Bible, a book which has been cherished and respected for centuries, would most likely be banned under a socialist-dominated government, and the possession of a copy of God's Word would likely become a crime. The freedom of an individual to practice, share, and proclaim their faith would be criminalized, and those who refuse to comply would be ultimately imprisoned of killed. This has occurred repeatedly in socialist and communist countries resulting in the oppression and obliteration of mass segments of national populations.

The right to ownership of property and businesses would be eliminated under a socialist-controlled government, and regardless of the message that ownership of businesses would be deferred to the population, that ownership would eventually wind up in the hands of the State, and would be managed, operated, and controlled by the State.

As freedoms and rights are dissolved away, the freedom to speak out and disagree with the government, which actively assails those rights and freedoms, would become a crime. In many universities and colleges in America today, the freedom of speech and assembly for Christian students has been eliminated in spite of the protection of those freedoms under the United Stated Constitution, and in most cases, no repercussions have been levied on the university leaders responsible. The removal of historical monuments and Christian symbols dedicated to the memory and honor of those who have served this nation are evidence to the arrogant attitude of the socialist mentality. Nothing in the Constitution prohibits a monument in the form of a Christian symbol from being in place in the public. And monuments to individuals who served in capacities which may be viewed as rebellious are not symbols of oppression. Many people forget that the American Civil War erupted out of the federal government's interference with rights which were delegated to the states, and while some practices of certain states were indeed deplorable and shrouded in injustice toward certain races in society, not all individuals who fought in that terrible war were in favor of those practices.

The Constitution of the United States serves to establish the structure of the Federal Government, dictate the means by which it operates, define specific irrevocable rights of the citizens under its authority, and identify its specific roles in ruling the nation. All authority which is not specifically regulated to the federal government as stated in the Constitution is deferred to the states which have the right to deal with those matters in accordance to the will of the majority of those state's citizens.

During the twentieth century, many states took a stand against the attacks on traditional marriage, only to have their voice silenced by secular, federally appointed judges in direct violation of the United States Constitution.

Finally, as the precious freedoms of American society set in place by the Constitution are slowly eradicated by socialism, a society and culture will come to pass where the American population will be forced under the threat of harsh consequences to comply with the rules and policies set forth by a socialist-controlled government, and the freedom to speak out against those rules and policies, along with the freedom of the citizens to effectively defend themselves against the government which would set those policies into effect, will become a thing of the past.

Tragically, the promises offered by socialism will never become a reality. Instead, a nation of poverty, oppression, government-initiated violence against opponents or dissidents, an unsustainable economy, and an unachievable system of medical care will be set into place, and once such a government is firmly seated in power, as history has proven, it will be extremely difficult, if not impossible, to remove. The only beneficiaries of socialism will be the socialist leaders who have deceived their way into power and authority; a power and authority which as time and history has shown will never surrender of its own free will despite the results of the will and actions of the nation's citizens. Those who currently flock to the platforms of socialist proponents have not taken a close look at history and its record of socialist tragedies, such as the Berlin Wall, the massacres of thousands of individuals in Cambodia, the violent response by China to the protesters in Tiananmen Square, the bread lines in Moscow, the empty shelves in the stores of Venezuela, the bodies of the thousands who have attempted to flee the past communist oppressions in Cuba, the starving populations of Zimbabwe, and the out-of-control corruption in Central America.

The stark reality is that socialism has never worked in any nation in which it has been instituted, and socialism has been responsible for the deaths of over one hundred million people. It should be remembered that Karl Marx, the individual who gave birth to the concept of socialism, was a failure in every sense of the word when it came to providing for the needs of his family.

In a 2018 article published by Doctor Lee Edwards, socialism is described as a pseudo-religion grounded in pseudoscience and enforced by political tyranny. No statement could be more accurate. The ultimate question is this: Will America embrace socialism's lies and atrocities, or endeavor to defend against them?

Through the establishment of a democratic government set forth in a priceless document known as the United States Constitution, the American people have been given something which has been denied to countless individuals around the world and throughout the years: a choice. The choice to accept or reject, the choice to succumb or resist, the choice to pursue freedom or accept oppression. A choice which is unavoidable and will be made sooner or later, either openly or passively. If American citizens truly desire to preserve a nation in which their children can grow up free with the opportunity to gain and achieve success in accordance with their hard work and abilities, American citizens will have to make a choice, and that choice ultimately lies in the individuals who are chosen to lead this nation.

The United States of America has been, is, and has the potential to continue to be a great nation. A nation that, while far from perfect, like any nation, has proven itself to be a nation which stands for freedom and justice. And though over the course of its history American leadership has made its share of mistakes, America has through its blessings, values, and efforts made a difference in a violent and troubled world. Its system of government has established more freedoms than those enjoyed by any other population on Earth. But only time will tell if America's citizens will elect to allow the government of the people, by the people, and for the people to become a government…of the government, by the government, and for the government. The ultimate choice is up to the people who make up this nation.

The United States of America's future, like its beginning, lies in the hearts and desires of its citizens. The fire of desire to be free and to live one's life without the dark shadow of tyranny looming over our nation day after day was first kindled in the hearts of our nation's Founding Fathers who risked their very lives to break the yoke of totalitarian rule and move on to create a nation where all people are created equal, have equal rights under the law, and have the protection of a government bound by a system of checks and balances to prevent the emergence of absolute authority in the hands of a handful of individuals.

On a regular basis, our nation holds elections in which American citizens have the opportunity to cast their vote for the candidate they feel is best suited to represent them and lead the nation. But one must remember that when casting a vote in the favor of an individual, it is important to know what that individual truly represents and desires to accomplish with the power entrusted to them. Rather than arbitrarily marking a ballot, Americans must take a moment to take a hard look into the past history of those candidates who are seeking, pushing, and enticing for a voter's approval. Is the candidate who is waving the proverbial carrot in front of you sincere, or are they a wolf in sheep's clothing? What is their history? How have they voted in the past? Where have they truly stood on the issues of concern to American society? When they speak, do they speak from facts, from speculation, or from false information?

Many political leaders today adamantly stomp their feet and complain to those who question their convictions that they are not socialists, but their actions, efforts, and attitudes dictate otherwise. For decades, children have been enthralled with the fairy tale story of Cinderella, from which an often-used adage has emerged over the years: If the shoe fits—wear it!

For the United States of America to remain a democracy, its people must carefully and consistently elect leaders who are faithful to their word, faithful to their obligation to speak for the people (not for themselves), and faithful to the Constitution of the United States of America as it is written. Even now, individuals who openly declare themselves as socialists are seated in the Congress of the United States and more are attempting to gain access to a voice in American government. If socialist individuals continue to be entrusted with the governing of the nation, it is only a matter of time before America crosses the edge of oblivion and falls into the chaos, oppression, and desolation of a nation in the death grip and oppression of socialism.

The blessings of security which America has enjoyed over the years have made its citizens complacent and indifferent to the dark threats which loom just over the legislative horizon. Today's generation, which has no first-hand experience at seeing the catastrophic impact on people's lives across the world as socialism and communism crept, marched, or charged into a society and plated its oppressive roots cannot or will not comprehend the potential for the same such catastrophe to take place in America.

The United States of America is not a perfect nation, but it is a good nation. And its Constitution has stood for well over two hundred years as a protector of freedom for its citizens. But if the American people persist on voting into office governors, delegates, senators, representatives, and other leaders who arrogantly defy the Constitution and the limits it imposes on their authority, there will come a day when our nation finds itself with a group of leaders in place who couldn't care less about supporting and defending that Constitution and will sweep it away with the broom of oppression and tyranny, leaving in its wake a socialist-controlled government.

And with the passing of American government and society into the shadow of socialism, the blessings of freedom will become only a distant memory. There is an old saying which is quoted by many people: *"You don't know what you've got until it's gone."* If the American people would learn anything from the lessons of history, it should be this: Freedom, once it is lost, is difficult, costly, and almost impossible to regain. If our Founding Fathers, who risked their very lives to establish a nation founded on freedom, could look across the years at the looming threat of socialism in our nation today, they would surely cry out from their graves for the American people to stand up, speak up, and do what is necessary to ensure that the ship of American freedom is steered away from the course which is taking all of us every closer to the edge of oblivion. As one of our nation's past leaders once stated: *"Freedom is never more than one generation away from extinction. We didn't pass it to our children in the bloodstream. It must be fought for, protected, and handed on for them to do the same"* (Ronald Regan, Former President of the United States).

ABOUT THE AUTHOR

Charles K. Kelly is native of Pearl River County Mississippi. He attended Pearl River Central High School in Carriere, MS, graduating in 1983. Charles went on to attend what was then known as Pearl River Junior College in Poplarville, MS, and later transferred to the University of Mississippi where he graduated with a bachelor's of science degree in geology in 1988.

After working as an insurance agent for Liberty National Life for about six months, Charles enlisted in the United States Navy and served for twenty years as a submarine sonar technician/supervisor and naval instructor, completing one tour of duty on a ballistic missile submarine, three tours of duty on attack submarines, and two tours of duty as a naval instructor.

While on active duty, Charles completed a master's of arts in biblical studies with Trinity Theological Seminary located in Newburg, Indiana, and has served as a bi-vocational pastor for churches in Rhode Island, Virginia, and Mississippi.

Following his naval career, Charles retired from active duty in 2009 and worked as a technical writer for a shipyard subsidiary corporation in Newport News, Virginia. During that period, Charles was introduced to the world of law enforcement and served as an auxiliary deputy sheriff for the sheriff's department in Portsmouth, Virginia, after completing the department's training academy.

Eager to return home, in 2015 Charles applied for and was accepted for a law enforcement position in his hometown of Picayune, Mississippi. After completing one of Mississippi's law enforcement academies, Charles received his state certification and has served for nearly five years as a law enforcement officer.

Charles has been married for the past thirty-two years to the love of his life, the former Jill L. Quayle of Choctaw, Oklahoma, and they have been blessed with three wonderful children: Linda Ann, Kristina Marie, and Bradley Michael.

REFERENCES

"The Reformation." History.com Editors. April 11, 2009
<https://www.history.com/topics/reformation>

"Who Were the Pilgrims." Pilgrim Plantation. 2019.
<https://www.plimoth.org>

"The Mayflower Compact." Mayflower History.com. Caleb Johnson.
<http://mayflowerhistory.com>

"U.S. Constitution Ratified." History.com. November 24, 2009.
<https://www.history.com/this-day-in-history/u-s-constitution-ratified>

"Codemakers: History of the Navajo Code Talkers." *American History Magazine*. William R. Wilson. February 1997.
<https://www.historynet.com>

"First Amendment." Findlaw.com. 2019.
<https://www.law.cornell.edu/constitution/first amendment>

"Increasing Calls for Brian Sims to 'immediately resign' for Harassing Pro-lifers." Fox News.com. Caleb Parke. May 8, 2019
https://www.FoxNews.com

"The Abuse of Freedom of The Press Law Constitutional Administrative Essay." UKEssays.com.11 2013.<https://www.uniassignment.com/essay-isamples/law/the
abuse-of-the-press-law-constitutional-administrative-essay.php?vref=1>

"Oath of Enlistment for Military Service." The Balance Careers. Rod Powers. October 18, 2018. https://www.thebalancecareers.com

"Oath of Office." United States Senate. https://www.senate.gov

"Definition of Socialism." Merriam-Webster Dictionary. <https://www.merriam-webster.com/dictionary/socialism.

"Karl Marx." History.com Editors. History. A&E Television Networks. May 13, 2019. https://www.history.com/topics/germany/karl-marx

"The History Guide Lectures on Modern European Intellectual History Karl Marx, 1818-1883." The History Guide. Steven Kries. January 30, 2008. https://www.history guide.org/intellect/marx.html.

 "The Ten Planks of the Communist Manifesto." The Communist Manifesto. Laissez-fairerepublic.com. Karl Heinrich Marx. 1848. <http://laissez-fairerepublic.com/TenPlanks.html.

"Socialism and Its Characteristics, Pros, Cons, Examples, and Types." The Balance. Kimberly Armadeo. April 25, 2019. https://www.thebalance.com/socialism-types-pros-cons-examples-3305592

"The Politically Incorrect Guide to Socialism." Goodreads.com. Kevin E. Williamson. https://Goodreads.com/the politically incorrect guide to socialism.

Introduction to 19th-Century Socialism. Paul Brians. October 8, 2016. https://brians.wsu.edu/2016/10/12/introduction-to-19th-century-socialism/

"What is the difference between Communism and Socialism?" David Floyd.
May 8, 2019. https://www.investopedia.com
"The History of Socialism." The Week Staff. February 20, 2016.
<https://theweek.com/articles/606526/history-socialism>

"Russian Revolution." Editors of Encyclopedia Britannica. April 2, 2019
(Last Updated). <https://www.britannica.com/event/Russian-Revolution-of-
1917>

"Treaty of Versailles." History.com Editors. History. A&E Television
Networks. August 29, 2018 (Last Updated).
<https://www.history.com/topics/world-war-i/treaty-of-versailles-1>

"World War II Casualties." World War 2. October 4, 2009.
http://worldwar2-database.blogspot.com/2010/10/world-war-ii-
casualties.html

"Adolf Hitler." History.com Editors. History. May 8, 2019. A&E Television
Networks. https://www.history.com/topic/world-war-ii/adolf-hitler-1

"How Communism Took Over Eastern Europe After World War II."
Vladimir Dubinsky. The Atlantic. October 22, 2012. https://www.the
atlantic.com/international archive/2012/10/how-communism-took-over-
eastern-europe-after-world-war-II/263968/

"The Foresight of Patton." Robert Orlando. Front Page Magazine. June 23,
2014. https://www.frontpagemag.com/fpm/234351/foresight-patton-robert-
orlando

"Churchill Delivers Iron Curtain Speech." History.com Editors.
History/This Day in History. March 2, 2010. A&E Television Networks.
https://www.history.com/this-day-in-history/churchill-delivers-iron-curtain-
speech

"Why Socialism Failed." Mark J. Perry. Foundation for Economic
Education. March 31, 1995. https://fee.org/articles/why-socialism-failed/

"Benjamin Franklin Quotes." Goodreads. Goodreads, Inc. 2019. http://www.goodreads.com/author/quotes/289513/Benjamin_Franklin
"A Scientific Approach to Christianity." Robert W. Faid. New Leaf Press, 1990.

"George Westinghouse: Servant Leader, Inventor, Captain of Industry." Gary Hoover. Archbridge Institute. February 27, 2019. https://www.archbridgeinstitute.org/george-westinghouse-servant-leader-inventor-captain-of-inductry

"Casualties of Operation Market Garden." Rob Hopmans. WW2 Gravestone. Word Press, 2018. <https://ww2gravestone.com.casualties-of-operation-market-garden/

"Socialism's Bloody History Shows Millennials Should Think Twice Before Supporting It." Stella Morabito. The Federalist.com, 2016. https://the federalist.com/2016/03/15/socialisms-bloody-history-shows-millenials-should-think-twice-before-supporting-it/

"5 Ways Socialism Destroys Societies." John Hawkins. February 25, 2014. http://townhall.com/columnists/johnhawkins/2014/02/25/5-ways-socialism-destroys-societies-n1800086

"Timeline: a history of free speech." David Smith and Luc Torres. February 6, 2006. https://www.theguardian.com/media/2006/feb/05/religion.news.

"Loss of a Yankee SSBN." Kurdin, Igor – Captain First Rank (Ret.) and Grasdock, Wayne, Lt. Cmdr. USN. Fall 2005 Vol. 7 No. 5. https://www.public.navy.mil/subfor/underseawarfare magazine.

"House Divided Speech." Abraham Lincoln Online (Roy Pl Basler – editor). Copywrite 2018. http://www.abrahamlincolnonline.org.

"Immigrants Who Escaped Socialist Countries Warn the U.S." Brenda Krueger Huffman. August 14, 2012. https://businessinsider.com.

"Zimbabwes Coup, Venezuala's Default, and the Ongoing Failure of Socialism." Investors.com Editors. https://www.investors.com/politics/editorials/zimbabwes coup-venezuales-default-and-the-ongoing-failure-of-socialism.

"Robert Mugabe Biography." Biography.com Editors. Publisher: A&E Television Networks. April 2, 2014. https://www.biography.com/political-figure/robert-mugabe.

"Hugo Chavez Biography." Biography.com Editors. Biography.com. April 1, 2014. https://www.biography.com/political -figure/hugo-chavez.

"Venezuelans regret gun ban, 'a declaration of war against an unarmed population.'" Holly McKay, Fox News. Fox News.com. December 2014. https://www.foxnews.com/world/venezuelans-regret-gun-prohibition-we-could-have-defended-ourselves.

"From Venezuela to France, Socialism is Failing All Over the World." Carlos Sabino. Panam Post. Last Updated April 30, 2017. https://panampost.com/carlos-sabino/2017/04/27/socialism-is-failing-all-over-the-world.

Socialism in America. United States History. https://www.u-s-history.com/pages/h1669.html.

"The History of Socialism." The Week Staff. The Week. February 20, 2016, https://theweek.com/articles/606526/history-socialism

"The Heroic Tale of Operation Entebbe, Israel's Most Daring Rescue Mission." Gisely Ruiz. All That's Interesting. February 22, 2018. https://allthasinteresting.com

"Mother Teresa's 10 Most Compassionate Pro-Life Quotes." Life Defender Team | Sep 1, 2016 https://lifedefender.org/2016/09/mother-teresas-10-most-compassionate-pro-life-quotes/

"FBI Crime Stats Show an Armed Public Is a Safer Public." Howard Nemerov. June 3, 2010. PJ Media.https://pjmedia.com/blog/fbi-crime-stats-show-an-armed-public-is-a-safer-public/

"A List of the Deadliest Mass Shootings in Modern U.S. History." Eyder Peral. The Two Way. June 12, 2016. https://www.npr.org/sections/thetwo-way/2016/06/12/481768384/a-list-of-the-deadliest-mass-shootings-in-u-s-history

"New Drive to Disarm America." The Minutemen. On Target. November 1, 1963.

"San Francisco Officials Brand NRA a 'Domestic Terrorist Organization.'" Adam Shaw. Fox News. https://www.foxnews.com/politics/san-francisco-board-brands-nra-a-domestic-terrorist-organization

"Modern Sporting Rifle: Introduction." National Shooting Sports Foundation (NSSF). 2019. https://www.nssf.org/msr

"ATF Bureau of Alcohol, Tobacco, Firearms and Explosives. Firearms Guide – Identification of Firearms Within the Purview of the National Firearms Act." 2016. https://www.art.gov

"2020 Dems ramp up calls to mandate assault weapons buyback: 'All of them.'" Brooke Singman. Fox News.com. 2019. https://www.foxnews.com/politics/2020-dems-assault-weapons-buyback-all-of-them

"Amid Screams of 'Red Light!' Texting Driver Kills 2." Kate Seamons. Newser Staff. October 19,2015. https://news.yahoo.com

"No Prison for Little Falls Teen Who Killed 2 While Texting Behind Wheel." Zoe Peterson. Star Tribune. March 4, 2016. http://www.startribune.com

"Governor Newsom Signs Police Use of Force Bill." Tyler Hayden. August 21, 2019. https://www.independent.com

"California Governor Signs Bill Striking Down Law That Made It A Crime to Refuse Police Officer's Request for Help." Owen Daugherty. September 4, 2019. The Hill. https://thehill.com.

Is America Embracing the 10 Tenets of the Communist Manifesto. Brian Koenig. The New American. April 23, 2012. https://www/thenewamerican.com/economy/commentary/item/11092-is-america-embracing-the-10-tenets-of-the-communist-manifesto.

Socialist Party USA 2018-2019 Platform. https://www.socialistpartyusa.net/platform.

"School Resource Officer Stopped School Shooting, Authorities Say." Daniel Victor. The New York Times. May 17, 2018. https://wwwnytimes.com/2018//05/17/us/dixon-school-shooting,html.

"Lone Resource Officer's Quick Action Stopped the Maryland School Shooter Within Seconds." Carma Hassan and Saeed Ahmed. CNN. March 21.2018. https://www.cnn.com/2018/03/20/us/maryland-school-shooting-resource-officer-response-trnd/index.html.

"Hero Officer Stopped Florida School Shooter in 3 Minutes, Sheriff Says." Tribune Media Wire. News Channel 3. April 21, 2018. https://wreg.com/2018/04/21/hero-officer-stopped-florida-school-shooting-in-3-minutes-sheriff-says.

"What is Joe Biden's Net Worth?" Anne Sraders. The Street. April 29, 2019. https://www.thestreet.com.

"How Bernie Sanders, the Socialist Senator, Amassed a $2.5 Million Fortune." Chase Peterson-Withorn (Forbes Staff). Forbes. April 12, 2019. https://www.forbes.com.

"How Elizabeth Warren Built a $12 Million Fortune." Michela Tindera (Forbes Staff). August 20, 2019. Forbes. https://www.forbes.com

"Nancy Pelosi Net Worth." Celebrity Net Worth. 2019. https://www.celebritynetworth.com.

"Charles Schumer Net Worth." Celebrity Net Worth. 2019. https://www.celebritynetworth.com.

"Diane Feinstein Net Worth." Celebrity Net Worth. 2018. https://www.celebritynetworth.com.

"What is Beto O'Rourke's Net Worth?" Ann Schmidt. Fox Business. September 13, 2019. https://www.foxbusiness.com

"500.000 Falls From Ladders Annually, 97 Percent Occur at Home or on Farms." Industrial Safety & Hygiene News (ISHN). July 6, 2917. https://www.ishn.com.

United States Population. World Meters. 2019. https://www.worldmeters.info.

"U.S. Vehicle Deaths Topped 40,000 in 2017, National Safety Council Estimates." Nathan Bomey. USA Today. February 15, 2018. https://www.usatoday.com.

Occupational Safety and Health Administration (OSHA). United States Department of Labor. Commonly Used Standards. 2018. https://www.osha.gov.

National Center for Health Statistics. 2018. https://www.cdc.gov/nchs/fastats/deaths.htm.

"What You Can Do." UC Davis Health. 2019. https://health.usdavis.edu.

"American Gun Ownership: The Positive Impacts of Law-Abiding Citizens

Owning Firearms." Ammo.com. 2019. https://ammo.com/articles/gun-ownership-in-america 2019.

"The Coming Generation War." Niall Ferguson and Eyck Freymann. The Atlantic. May 26, 2019. https://www.theatlantic.comn/ideas/archive/2019/05/coming-generation war/588670/

"Most Millennials Would Vote For A Socialist Over A Capitalist, Poll Finds." Megan Henney. Fox Business News. October 29, 2019. https://www.foxbusiness.com/money/millennials-socialist-vote-capitalist-poll.

"This is Why Millennials Favor Socialism." Sean Vazquez. Searching for Logic. April 4, 2017. https://www.huffpost.com.

"14 Things Bernie Sanders Has Said About Socialism." Michael Kruse. Politico. July 17, 2015. https://www.politico.com/story.

"Bernie Sanders Says 'No' to Americans Who Want to Keep Private Insurance Under Medicare-for-All." Joseph A. Wulfsohn. Fox News. February 2015. https://www.foxnews.com/politics.

"Poll: Majority View Socialism as Incompatible with American Values." Jonathan Easley. The Hill. May 6, 2019. https://thehill.com/homenews/campaign.

"Sanders Seeks 'Concessions' from Gun Owners, Though 99.9% Would Never Commit Mass Shootings." Lukas Mikelionis. Fox News. 2019. https://www.foxnew.com/politics.

"What Americans Must Know About Socialism." Lee Edwards, Ph.D. Progressivism. December 3, 2018. https://www.heritage.org/progressivism/commentary.

"What the data says about gun deaths in the U.S." John Gramlich. Pew

Research. August 16, 2019. https://www.pewreasearch.org/fact-tank/2019/08/16/What-the-data-say-about-gun-deaths-in-the-u-s/

"Guns Prevent Thousands of Crimes Every Day, Research Shows." Lawrence W. Reed. Foundation for Economic Education (FFE). August 23, 2019. https://fee.org/articles/guns-prevent-thousands-of-crimes-every-day-research-show/

"The Ugly Truth About Socialism." Harry M. Williams. Perpetual Adoration. September 14, 2019. https://adoration.com/2019/the-ugly-truth-about-socialism/

Governor signs 5 pieces of gun control legislation into Virginia law. Cameron Thompson. News 6 Richmond. April 10, 2020. https://www.wtvr.com/news/virginia-politics/governor-signs-5-pieces-of-gun-control-legislation-into-virginia-law

"Michigan governor extends coronavirus state of emergency, but could face legal challenges." Jack Turman, Adam Brewster. May 1, 2020 CBS News https://www.cbsnews.com/news/michigan-stay-at-home-order-extended-gretchen-whitmer-state-of-emergency/